Rangers All-Time Greats

*Men who made
Ibrox history*

Rangers All-Time Greats

Men who made Ibrox history

SIENA

Above: Hearts keeper Gilles
Rousset thwarts Rangers striker
Gordon Durie.

Siena
PO Box 14840
London NW3 5WT

ISBN 0-75252-373-2

This independent publication
has been prepared without
any involvement on the part
of Rangers Football Club or
the Scottish Football League.

Contents

Introduction

At the beginning of the 1997-98 season, Glasgow Rangers FC stood on the verge of history. Having drawn level with city rivals Celtic's long-standing nine Championships in a row, they were poised to claim the record outright if they could only clinch that all-important tenth win.

While Celtic had been led to their record by the legendary Jock Stein, Rangers' manager Walter Smith was an altogether less charismatic figure. Indeed, his autobiography had been titled, with tongue in cheek one assumes, Mr Smith. He'd never made big headlines, having played for such unfancied teams as Dundee United and Dumbarton, and his management experience before coming to Ibrox as Graeme Souness' assistant was minimal. Yet his team had done the talking for him and an influx of talent on the coaching and playing sides in the summer of 1997 suggested he was reluctant to rest on his laurels.

Yet the problem remained that a Rangers side under Smith had yet to make its mark in Europe. That not only put it at a disadvantage compared with the side that won the European Cup Winners' Cup by beating Dynamo Moscow in 1972, but also kept it firmly in the shade when compared with Celtic's Lisbon Lions of 1967. That of course was the first team to bring the European Cup, the ultimate club prize, back to Britain.

For the best past of a decade the Scottish title had been Rangers' passport to that very competition – but aside from 1992-93, when they finished second to Marseille in a bid to make the Final, very little success had resulted. Indeed, embarrassing defeats in the early rounds to Grasshopper, AEK Athens and Steaua had resulted in Rangers' fans expecting just one trip abroad each season.

The problem was, of course, that to put all their energies into winning the European Cup they would

Right: Danish international Erik Bo Andersen was bought from Randers in 1996 as Rangers set their sights on Celtic's record.

run the risk of slipping up at home. It would take a long time to put together another nine in a row – and if the team to foil them were to sport green and white hoops, the discontent could readily be imagined. Only in Glasgow could second place be deemed failure – and that was something successive managers had been very much aware of.

ELDER STATESMEN

Rangers, the oldest of the two Glasgow giants by 16 years, had always set their sights high. At the end of their very first campaign, 1890-91, they shared the Championship with Dumbarton and would win the title outright on another 46 occasions. The players who brought them that success were almost all Scottish born and bred, but the arrival of Graeme Souness in 1986 made Glasgow football an altogether more cosmopolitan affair. His tactic of buying the best, regardless of nationality, has been continued by his successor Walter Smith and both managers' acquisitions are liberally represented here alongside earlier heroes.

The greats of the postwar era like man-mountain George Young are listed alongside Willie Waddell, who made the transition from winger to manager. Alan Morton, the 'wee blue devil' who tormented the English went on to become a director of the club, while Jock Wallace would hold the reigns for two spells in the 1970s and 1980s.

IBROX LEGEND

Yet anyone who says 'they don't make 'em, like that anymore' should take a long, hard look at Ally McCoist. The striker who returned to Scotland with his tail between his legs after an unsuccessful couple of seasons south of the border with Sunderland went on to beat Bob McPhail's goalscoring record that had stood since 1939. And in an era when football's biggest names seem prepared to follow the lure of easy money, he's remained a Rangers fixture despite his ins and outs with management to play a part in the bid for that tenth title. Even more recent players like Mark Hateley, Colin Stein, Derek Johnstone and Trevor Steven have returned to the club after spells elsewhere – such is the lure of Ibrox.

Graeme Souness went out of his way to stress that Glasgow football's traditional religious divide was no bar to buying talent when he signed ex-Celt Mo Johnston. And while that experiment was not a whole-hearted success, there's little doubt that Walter Smith's interest in a player majors on his on-field skills – not his off-field beliefs. In his quest to add European honours to Scottish domination, he's now assisted by a new Danish coach, while an interpreter might well be handy to make sure his team talks are fully understood by an influx of continental talent.

It's not impossible, given the strength of Rangers' 1997-98 playing squad, that they could field entirely different teams for Scottish and European matches. Not that it's likely to happen – but strength in depth is always a Smith priority. How many of the names on his team sheet will make it into a second volume of All-Time Greats remains to be seen – the likes of Erik Bo Andersen only just missed out this time round – but any player who plays his part in winning a tenth title will have staked a mighty claim.

Above: Star striker Mark Hateley celebrates his equaliser against Dundee in 1993. The former England international would enjoy five title-winning seasons at Ibrox.

7

Rangers Club History

Europe's talent to the blue half of Glasgow, underlined the fact that chairman David Murray intended to maintain their pre-eminent position in Scottish football and extend it to the continent.

The name of Glasgow Rangers first came to public attention in 1873 when the club was founded by a group of rowing enthusiasts. They played their first games on numerous different pitches, including an area of parkland known as Flesher's Haugh and then Kinning Park, before opening their first Ibrox Park in 1887 (the current Ibrox was built on a nearby patch of land some 12 years later).

THE OLD FIRM

Though Queens Park were the power in the land, a more intense rivalry that sprung up was with another Glasgow neighbour, Celtic. Indeed, the pair had locked horns in Celtic's very first match in May 1888. Against the odds, it was the side in green that ran out 5-2 winners – Rangers having reportedly contributed to their own downfall by 'doing a Queen's Park' and fielding a reserve team. The crowd was some 2,000 strong, women being admitted free and others paying sixpence a head. Yet the most fascinating fact must surely be that the two sets of players chose to wind down together by sharing tea in a local hall. Hardly the image of the fixture in more recent years…

The Scottish League opened for business in 1890-91, and Rangers were quickly out of the blocks, sharing the very first title with Dumbarton. September 1898's meeting with Celtic had attracted a crowd of 44,868 – underlining the fact that the 'Old Firm' rivalry, as it became known, was already highly profitable in terms of bodies through the turnstiles.

When Glasgow Rangers first opened for business in the late nineteenth century, the dominant team in Scottish football was Queen's Park, a team of devoted amateur gentlemen, and it was symbolic of Rangers' position that their more established opponents sent their reserve team, quaintly named the Strollers, to play them. Now, Queen's Park languish in the Third Division while Rangers have 47 Championships to their name.

The change in status reflects not only the inevitable rise of professionalism but the determination of Rangers – motto 'Ready' – to be the best. Their Ibrox Stadium is the envy of clubs the world over, with a current capacity of some 50,000 in all-seater comfort, and the spending spree of summer 1997, which saw manager Walter Smith breaking the bank to bring the cream of

ALAN MORTON
GLASGOW RANGERS

WILLS'S CIGARETTES

J. DAWSON (RANGERS)

Left: Nicknamed the 'wee blue devil', Alan Morton would win nine Championships during his 13 years with Rangers before his retirement in 1932.

Right: Goalkeeper Jerry Dawson – who made his 'Old Firm' debut the day his opposite number John Thompson was fatally injured – served the Ibrox club from 1929-45.

Opposite: Forever synonymous with Rangers, wing-half John Greig enjoyed 18 years as a player and would go on to manage the club for five years.

Above: Celtic captain Billy McNeill and his Rangers counterpart John Greig lead their teams out for the 1973 Scottish Cup Final. Goals from Parlane, Conn and Forsyth would send the blue half of Glasgow into raptures with a 3-2 victory.

It was clear, too, that the old order, in the shape of Queen's Park, was about to change in the face of the dual domination from the blue and green. The first Old Firm clash in the Scottish Cup had taken place in 1890, and they met again in the Final four years later when Rangers ran out winners by three goals to one. The sides would meet once more in the Final in 1899, with Celtic this time taking delight in depriving their rivals of a first League and Cup Double.

Nevertheless, Rangers were in the ascendant at the turn of the century, with four League titles in a row. The season of 1898-99 was particularly memorable, in that it saw the Gers win all 18 games to establish a perfect record. But Celtic then took over, and though Rangers had the chance to foil a third League and Cup Double in 1909,

the Scottish FA withheld the Cup due to disgraceful scenes after a pitch invasion by drink-fuelled hordes. The 'Hampden Riot' had written itself a sorry page in the history books, and both clubs were ordered to compensate hosts Queen's Park for the damage caused by their so-called fans.

Rangers went into the war years with colours flying, returning three successive title seasons to end Celtic's six in a row. Football north of the border continued through the First World War, though the Scottish Cup was suspended and players' wages reduced to £2 a week. Rangers took the last wartime crown by a single point and would hold the whip hand between the wars with 15 title wins to Celtic's five. The Glasgow stranglehold was such that through the 1920s the pennant never left the city.

CUP HAT-TRICK

Rangers' managerial regime was very stable: Bill Struth, a former player, became the club's first secretary-manager after secretary William Wilton drowned in 1920. By the time of his retirement in 1954, Struth had gathered 18 League titles, reached 10 Cup Finals and two League Cup Finals.

The key statistic of the 1930s was three consecutive Scottish Cup wins from 1934-36. History was there to be made in 1937 when they set out on the trail of a fourth win, only to lose in the First Round to lowly Queen of the South. Ironically, this was the first Rangers game ever to be immortalised on film!

The postwar seasons saw Rangers well on top, but not before a boardroom coup in the summer of 1947. The board of Rangers had previously been an amateur body made up of former players, but when chairman Jimmy

Bowie suggested Bill Struth stand down, a revolution occurred. In many ways, this was the first stage of a process that would lead to the club's purchase by David Murray in 1988.

The 1948-49 season brought an historic 'treble' of League, Cup and League Cup never before achieved, the success based on the so-called 'Iron Curtain' defence which remained virtually unchanged from 1946 to 1953. Another purple patch began at the end of the 1950s: from 1957 until 1965, Rangers achieved four League titles, plus an equal number of wins in both League and FA Cups. This was the era of 'Slim Jim' Baxter, a superb ballplayer who was by turns exhilarating and exasperating.

But though Baxter was to depart for England in 1965, there was a player who had been a first-team regular for the past couple of seasons who would mature into an inspirational leader, a stalwart in the dark blue of Scotland

Below: Davie Cooper, a local legend after more than a decade at Ibrox and one who would be mourned by the whole of Scotland after his untimely death at the age of 39.

Left: The face of Ibrox before the days of all-seater stadia.

Above: The triumphant Rangers team after the 1984 League Cup Final that brought a 3-2 victory over Celtic.

Opposite: Sandy Clark was brought from West Ham Utd to aid Ally McCoist in the hunt for goals but would make just 43 League appearances.

and would eventually manage the club. John Greig was that man, and though Rangers would play out the decade in the shadow of their European Cup-winning neighbours, the foundations were being laid for future success.

This would not however be achieved under long-serving boss Scot Symon, who had replaced Bill Struth in 1954. He paid the penalty of Celtic's success in Scotland and Europe in October 1967, giving way to his former assistant Davie White who would in turn be replaced two years later. Willie Waddell, who'd brought the Championship to lowly Kilmarnock in 1965, made an immediate mark when the League Cup was secured by a single Derek Johnstone goal in 1970. The new man was to step upstairs in 1972, handing over responsibility for playing matters to Jock Wallace, but would prove a rock in the months to come.

CROWD CATASTROPHE

The old adage, attributed to Bill Shankly, that 'football's not a matter of life and death…it's more important than that' was shown to be false by the tragic events at Ibrox on 2 January 1971. The traditional New Year's Day fixture had been postponed for 24 hours to the Saturday to give an extra day's break from Hogmanay hangovers, and the 80,000 crowd was well behaved.

With Celtic marginally in the lead, many Rangers fans decided to head home before the final whistle. Yet cheers from the crowd in the stadium on Colin Stein's last-gasp equaliser had the effect of reversing the flow of the exodus, with disastrous results. Sixty-six lives were lost that day, uniting the city of Glasgow in grief. Willie Waddell was horrified by the tragedy: he orchestrated the club's response, ensuring players were at every funeral, and it was largely thanks to his perseverance and vision that Ibrox was redeveloped in a manner that made it, however belatedly, a state of the art stadium with spectator comfort and safety at its core.

Jock Wallace's drive boosted blue fortunes on the pitch, especially when the Gers grabbed their own long-awaited share of European glory in Barcelona's Nou Camp stadium in 1972. The triumph was tainted by crowd trouble, exacerbated by the fact that, 3-0 up against Dynamo Moscow, Rangers lost concentration and ended up hanging on grimly to a 3-2 lead at the final whistle. A pitch invasion, however well-intentioned, by relieved Rangers fans was repelled by a baton charge and the resulting scenes of violence, broadcast live across Europe, ended with a European ban, originally for two years but bartered down to one. This, however, denied the players

who'd fought so hard to make their European mark the chance to defend their title. Their defeat of Bayern Munich in particular had been remarkable, winning through despite the absence of the injured Greig.

On the domestic front, a League Cup win over Celtic in 1971, when Wallace was coach, followed by victory in the Centenary Cup Final in 1973, had suggested better times to come – and three titles in 1975, 1976 and 1978, the last two Doubles, proved that the pendulum was indeed swinging as Jock Stein left the Glasgow scene. Jock Wallace gave way to John Greig, who found himself taking charge just as a century of history was about to be turned on its head. The Glasgow giants had been caught by the passage of time, and what some commentators coined 'a New Firm' of Aberdeen and Dundee United had emerged to challenge the big city's dominance.

Greig's five years at the helm brought cups but no League title, and he resigned after just a few games of the 1983-84 season, his last major act having been to sign Ally McCoist from Sunderland. Former Ibrox favourite Alex Ferguson, the man who'd driven Aberdeen to glory, turned down a return in a managerial capacity, so Jock Wallace was granted a second spell. As so often happens, it was not to prove as profitable as the first, and Rangers ended 1985-86 with fewer points than games: fifth place was their equal worst postwar showing.

A January 1986 takeover of the club by the John Lawrence construction company brought fresh faces into the boardroom, and it was inevitable that change would eventually permeate down the club's structure to pitch level. Jock Wallace resigned, to be replaced by the first player-manager in Rangers' history. Graeme Souness, fresh from a trophy-studded career with Liverpool and latterly in Italy, broke the 'Old Firm' mould in more ways than one. Most importantly of all, he'd dismantle Rangers' 'no Catholics' policy at a single stroke in July with the recruitment of Maurice Johnston, the high-profile Celtic striker who'd more recently played in France.

ANGLO INVASION

Souness' arrival at Ibrox in April 1986 heralded an amazing turnround in the club's fortunes – but he was forced to admit defeat on one front. His intention to pursue a playing role was too high-pressure to sustain, especially for a whole-hearted and combative midfielder. This became apparent in August 1987 when he spoke out of turn to the referee and was sent off, having committed a second bookable offence. He continued his argument after the game, winning himself a fine from the SFA and confirming what many had thought. His forays on the pitch had tapered down to six subs' appearances by 1988-89, compared with 25 and 18 games in previous seasons.

Souness struck gold in what was his first season in management, aided by a stream of high-quality (and often high-priced) players from south of the border. Terry Butcher and Chris Woods, both regulars in the England rearguard, patrolled the penalty area with fellow international Graham Roberts, while the likes of McCoist and Fleck popped in the goals up front. A Championship and League Cup Double was an impressive start, but despite the arrival of the likes of Richard Gough, Trevor Francis and Ray Wilkins, only the League Cup could be retained the following term.

The teams Souness selected took no prisoners, but the 'Old Firm' clash of 17 October 1987 was memorable for events that ended not with the final whistle but in a court of law. Woods, McAvennie and Butcher had all been dismissed for violent conduct during the game, while Roberts was also implicated. Woods and Butcher were found guilty in what was the first example of the Scottish legal system involving itself in matters on the pitch.

If Rangers matches were more eventful these days than ever before, results certainly reflected a growing feeling that the Gers were on the march. The Championship returned in 1988-89, the League Cup staying in the Ibrox trophy room for a club record third season. Maurice Johnston's arrival, as previously mentioned, grabbed most of the headlines in summer 1989, but Trevor Steven's arrival to play on the right of midfield was crucial in ensuring the club's second title.

Souness departed after Championship number four of his reign, but the title battle with Aberdeen had gone right down to the wire: a League Cup Final win against Celtic was the icing on the cake.

If the manager's decision to return to his spiritual home, Anfield, had been an unpleasant shock, at least the Ibrox directors didn't have far to look for a replacement: Walter Smith, though he had no previous managerial form, was well capable of taking the reins and building on what had already been achieved.

Below: Former England international Terry Butcher was brought in to add steel to the Gers' back four.

The Club Today

I f Graeme Souness' Ibrox reign had set everything on its head, his shock departure in 1991 to return to Anfield threw Ibrox into turmoil. (Ironically, it was ex-Celt Kenny Dalglish's equally unexpected exit that had opened the vacancy.) Sensibly, the board nominated his assistant Walter Smith as his successor, and the wisdom of that decision is shown by the fact that they kicked off the 1997-98 season looking for their tenth consecutive title. As supporters of both sides barely needed telling, this would eclipse Celtic's record set in the Jock Stein era.

While the Celtic board went through managers as if discarding playing cards – Glasgow was hardly the place to learn the managerial ropes – Smith, backed by chairman David Murray's millions, quietly continued attracting the cream of Europe's footballing talent to Ibrox. A rapid outflow of Souness' Englishmen in Woods, Steven and Walters was replaced by another trio from south of the border in Goram, McCall, and Gordon, while Rideout replaced Everton-bound Mo Johnston – a gamble that had not really come off.

One player already on the staff to shine in Souness' absence was Ally McCoist. Relegated to the bench so often in recent years he must have had splinters, Super Ally was a man reborn and proved it with a career best 41-goal haul that almost single-handedly guaranteed

Right: Manager Walter Smith continued the winning run that had begun under his predecessor.

Opposite: Goal machine Ally McCoist has been a fixture at Ibrox for nearly 15 years and has played a major part in Rangers' renaissance.

18

Above: Midfielder Stuart McCall was one of Smith's first acquisitions as manager.

Rangers their fourth title in a row. The fifth would be part of a golden Treble, in 1992-93, that underlined the fact that Walter Smith had not only carried on the Souness era but built on it.

MAKING HIS MARK

The player who survived the 'purge' of Englishmen to prove a match-winner in the Smith era was Mark Hateley. Son of former Liverpool striker Tony, he overcame fan antipathy to prove a mightily effective spearhead. Indeed it was his second goal against Aberdeen, their nearest challengers in the League, that made the Cup safe. It was

to be the Dons who ran Rangers closest in 1993-94, but Hateley once again proved talismanic, his 42 appearances yielding 22 vital goals.

The Englishman's contribution was made even more vital by the fact that Ally McCoist was just one member of a spiralling injury list. Having broken a leg while on Scotland duty, he came back to score a dream decider in what was, incredibly, Rangers' seventh League Cup Final in eight years, leaving opponents Hibs distraught as the chance of extra time was snatched from their grasp.

Equally last-gasp was Rangers' hunt for the Treble. Opponents Dundee United had not enjoyed the best of seasons, but a single goal sent the underdogs back to Tannadice Park rejoicing. Some blamed reserve keeper Ally Maxwell for the upset, but in truth he was sold short by a Dave McPherson backpass, and it may have been no coincidence that Big Mac was on his way back to Hearts shortly after the season's end. Europe had seen them lose out to Levski Sofia in the First Round through something of a freak goal.

Smith strengthened his team in customary fashion during the summer of 1994, but the close season saw him pull off a transfer that had the world sitting up and taking notice. Great Dane Michael Laudrup was the man who would consistently turn on the flair to keep the Ibrox faithful in ecstasies, and his match-winning performances were rewarded with both the Scottish PFA and Football Writers' Player of the Year Awards in 1995. Such was Rangers' dominance of the domestic scene that Smith was able to afford the odd high-profile mistake, such as French stopper Basile Boli, who proved a less than impressive replacement for McPherson.

EUROPEAN ANGUISH

The 1994-95 season was something of a cakewalk for the blues, only Motherwell putting up any Championship

Left: Brian Laudrup was bought as Rangers strengthened their grip on the Premier Division title and aimed for success in Europe.

Above: Dutch international Peter Van Vossen, pictured during a Rangers training session.

resistance but being left a whopping 15 points in the Ibrox team's wake. It was becoming a recurring pattern that while Rangers were far too good for Scottish opposition they were unable to stamp that same authority on the European game. The departure from the Champions Cup against AEK Athens happened in August, of all times, and cast something of a shadow over the forthcoming season. Analysis of the team sheets revealed no fewer than 33 names, but the backbone of the season was a 15-game unbeaten run that started with a 3-1 win over Celtic at their temporary home, Hampden Park.

DOMESTIC DOMINATION

Rangers completed their third Double of the 1990s in 1995-96 and, with three wins and three draws, showed they were very much the masters in 'Old Firm' terms despite the return of ex-Celt Tommy Burns to Parkhead as manager.

England playmaker Paul 'Gazza' Gascoigne was the man who made everything tick. Gordan Petric and Stephen Wright were also recruited to stiffen the centre and right of the defence and add options to a squad that Walter Smith utilised in a continental 3-5-2 formation, wing-backs pressing into midfield in an attempt to play the foreigners at their own game.

In the absence of Pieter Huistra, bound for the Japanese J-League, Smith had added attacking flair of the Continental kind in Oleg Salenko. The player, a Russian international who'd hit a record five for his country in a World Cup match with Cameroon, was a consolation prize after the intended capture, Romania's Florin Raduciouiu, escaped the Ibrox net. In January 1996, Rangers replaced him with Dutchman Peter Van Vossen (in an exchange deal) and Denmark's Erik Bo Andersen, who'd created a big reputation with Aalborg.

Those players were vital additions to a squad that again was ravaged by injury, notably the striking pair of McCoist and Gordon Durie. Had Smith appreciated that the duo would be stricken this way, it's certain he'd have retained Mark Hateley, who left to help former team-mate Ray Wilkins in his attempt to prevent Queens Park Rangers' relegation from the top flight. Hateley would return from his fruitless stay south of the border to aid the

Left: English enigma Paul Gascoigne, imported from Italy in 1995, was rewarded for his part in Rangers' 1990s success with a new contract despite being dogged by off-field controversy.

Gers during the last few months of the 1996-97 campaign.

The retention of the Championship pennant was crucial to all at Ibrox, for it would ensure Rangers a share of the nine-in-a-row record held by their city rivals. No sooner was the ninth consecutive title under their belt than Rangers were making clear their plans for the future. A vote of confidence was placed in the current managerial team of Walter Smith and Archie Knox by extending their contracts until the millenium, ensuring continuity of leadership.

CONTINENTAL CLASS

Just as important though was the May 1997 appointment of Dane Tommy Moller-Nielsen, son of former national team manager Richard, as first-team coach. Chairman David Murray explained his thinking was very much on the European campaign to come, and improving Rangers' disappointing recent record in that respect. 'It's one thing saying we are a big club,' he pointed out, 'it is quite another thing going and doing it.'

Moller-Nielsen revealed he'd been following Rangers for 15 years. 'The connection came though Kai Johanneson, a former Rangers player, who was friendly with my dad,' he explained.

With Mark Hateley departing for a player-manager post with Hull City and Alan McLaren's knee operation likely to keep him out of the start of the new season – injury having plagued him seven months of 1996-97 – it was clear that Walter Smith would be casting an eye over the transfer market in order to strengthen his squad. Despite the possibility of a tenth consecutive title, the European Cup also loomed large in Smith's plans. Kicking off their campaign against Faroe Island Champions GI Gotu, Rangers would also need to dispose of Swedes Gothenburg before they could enter the group stages.

The names on display in 1997-98 – Amoruso (from Fiorentina) and Stensaas (from Rosenborg) were two more summer signings – would not instantly be familiar to the Ibrox faithful. Whether they could conquer Europe while eclipsing their rivals' title ambitions at home remained to be seen. Yet, as ever, anyone wearing that famous shirt and putting their all into it would be hailed as a conquering hero…and a potential All-Time Great.

Left: Defender Craig Moore has become a familiar figure to the Ibrox crowds following his arrival from the Australian Institute of Sport.

Player Profiles

There have been many talented individuals who have displayed their skills and enthralled Ibrox crowds over the years. This book hopefully brings you closer, in words and pictures, to some of the most celebrated players ever to have represented the club. But have you thought about what you could do if you could select from all those featured?

Imagine Alan Morton feeding crosses from the wing for a twin strike force of McCoist and Stein to convert… or a back four of Gough, Jackson, Young and Caldow? The legendary Waddell could link in midfield with Gazza, or we could turn back the clock to field inspirational captain Grieg alongside the experienced Wilkins.

All in all, the possibilities are endless, except in the goalkeeping department where just three custodians vie for the shirt. But even then, how do you choose between 1972 hero McCloy and England international Woods? We'll leave it up to you!

1960-1965 & 1969-1970

Jim Baxter

PERSONAL FILE

Born: 29 September 1939
Birthplace: Hill of Beath, Fife
Height: 5' 10"
Weight: 10st 6lb

LEAGUE RECORD

FROM-TO	CLUB	APPS	GOALS
1957-60	Raith Rovers	n/k	n/k
1960-65	Rangers	136	18
1965-67	Sunderland	87	10
1967-69	Nott'm Forest	48	3
1969-70	Rangers	14	1
Total		285	32

RANGERS LEAGUE DEBUT

24 August 1960 v Partick Thistle

SCOTLAND DEBUT

9 November 1960 v Northern Ireland

SCOTLAND HONOURS

SEASON	CAPS
1960-61	4
1961-62	6
1962-63	7
1963-64	4
1964-65	3
1965-66	6
1966-67	3
1967-68	1
Total	34

DID YOU KNOW?
In just five seasons Jim Baxter won three League Championship, three Scottish Cup and four League Cup medals.

Few Rangers players, past or present, have attracted the praise that 'Slim' Jim Baxter deservedly amassed in five glorious years at Ibrox. Probably the most gifted and cultured left-sided player to turn out for the club, James Curran Baxter remains a figure of worship for Rangers supporters – even to those who never saw him play.

Fife-born Baxter was prised from Raith Rovers by manager Scot Symon in June 1960 for a then Scottish transfer record fee of £17,500. Baxter's productive partnership with inside-forward Ian McMillan laid the foundations for one of Rangers' most successful sides that dominated the early part of the Swinging Sixties.

And no one exemplified the freewheelin' decade north of the border with more flair than Baxter, who helped his side win 10 of the 15 domestic prizes on offer, despite having only a passing interest in serious defending from the centre of the park. Baxter collected more honours during his time at Rangers than most players do in their entire career and represented Scotland with great success, particularly against the English.

In 1963, Baxter bagged both goals as a ten-man Scotland outfit beat Alf Ramsey's men 2-1 at Wembley. In the same year, his talent was given a larger stage as he represented a European XI against England in the Football Association Centenary match, again at Wembley.

Baxter headed south in May 1965 to sign for Sunderland for a fee of £72,500 and two years later joined Nottingham Forest for £100,000, but neither move could be described as successful. His return to Ibrox for a season was unimpressive and his decline, due to an over-fondness for alcohol, was as rapid as it was sad and he was lost to the game he graced so magnificently.

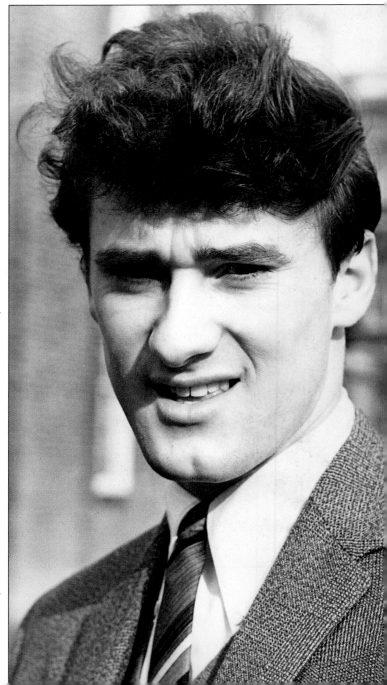

Terry Butcher

PERSONAL FILE

Born: 28 December 1958
Birthplace: Singapore
Height: 6' 4"
Weight: 14st 0lb

LEAGUE RECORD

FROM-TO	CLUB	APPS	GOALS
1976-86	Ipswich Town	271	16
1986-90	Rangers	127	9
1990-92	Coventry	6	—
1992-93	Sunderland	38	—
Total		442	25

RANGERS LEAGUE DEBUT

9 August 1986 v Hibernian

ENGLAND DEBUT

31 May 1980 v Australia

ENGLAND HONOURS

SEASON	CAPS
1979-80	1
1980-81	1
1981-82	6
1982-83	11
1983-84	5
1984-85	11
1985-86	10
1986-87	7
1987-88	2
1988-89	9
1989-90	14
Total	77

DID YOU KNOW?

As well as commentating for radio, Terry Butcher runs a hotel in Bridge of Allen near Stirling.

Big Terry Butcher was Graeme Souness' second significant signing, as the former Scotland captain sought to secure Rangers' right to be hailed a major British footballing force. The England central defender was enticed north by Rangers' first ever player-manager for £725,000 in August 1986 from Ipswich Town – just two months after his international goalkeeping team-mate Chris Woods joined the ranks from Norwich City for £600,000.

Despite a losing start to his Rangers career, 2-1 against Hibernian at Easter Road where Souness was sent off, Butcher's impact over the season was significant and he led his team to a League Championship and League Cup success.

Butcher was involved in a court case in 1987, along with Woods and Celtic's Frank McAvennie, following a bad-tempered affair at Ibrox. The Rangers pair were fined £250, which was upheld on appeal and almost soured their love affair with Scotland forever. However, both were persuaded to stay on and gather more silverware for the Ibrox trophy cabinet.

The towering six-foot-four-inch Butcher's dominance at the heart of the defence enabled Gers to win two more League titles plus another League Cup. He also skippered England during Italia '90, where his side were beaten in the World Cup Semi-Finals by eventual winners Germany.

After his relationship with Souness cooled, Butcher returned south in 1990 to become player-manager of Coventry City, but his tenure was relatively short and unsuccessful and a brief spell with Sunderland saw his playing career brought to an end.

Eric Caldow

DID YOU KNOW?
Eric Caldow won 29 of his Scottish caps at left-back, the remainder on the other flank.

Arriving at Ibrox in the summer of 1952 via the Glenpark and Muirkirk junior teams, full-back Eric Caldow would soon make himself an indispensable part of the light blue scene. For the next 14 seasons he would star as either right or left back, translating his sterling club form into 40 caps for his country.

He might have had more but for an appalling

injury in the 1963 Home International against England, the thrice-broken leg sustained minutes into the game after a clash with Bobby Smith thus ending his international career. Prior to this, he'd only been absent twice in six years, and for half that time had captained the Scotland side as he did Rangers.

A master of the defence-splitting pass, Caldow would instigate as many Rangers attacks as he would break down those of the opposition: he was also a ferocious tackler despite being less than strongly built, and was fast on his feet. His Ibrox tenure saw him play a part in two fine teams – having started off in the era of Young, McColl and Waddell, by the time he retired the likes of Greig, Johnston and McKinnon had emerged to carry the club to further glory. His honours on retirement amounted to five League titles plus three League and two FA Cup wins.

Caldow soldiered on for three more seasons after his injury, regaining a regular spot in late 1964 before moving to Stirling Albion for one last fling. He would retain his contact with the game as manager of Stranraer and latterly as a scout for Queens Park Rangers. A cool head when others were losing theirs, Eric Caldow was never once dismissed during his career.

Davie Cooper

PERSONAL FILE

Born: 25 February 1956
Birthplace: Hamilton
Died 23 March 1995
Height: 5' 8"
Weight: 12st 5lb

LEAGUE RECORD

FROM-TO	CLUB	APPS	GOALS
1974-77	Clydebank	90	28
1977-89	Rangers	377	49
1989-94	Motherwell	157	17
1994-95	Clydebank	21	1
Total		645	95

RANGERS LEAGUE DEBUT

13 August 1977 v Aberdeen

SCOTLAND DEBUT

12 September 1979 v Peru

SCOTLAND HONOURS

SEASON	CAPS
1979-80	2
1980-81	—
1981-82	—
1982-83	—
1983-84	2
1984-85	5
1985-86	7
1986-87	4
1987-88	—
1988-89	—
1989-90	2
Total	22

DID YOU KNOW?
On the night of Jock Stein's passing, Davie scored the penalty which virtually ensured Scotland's World Cup qualification.

Davie Cooper was not only one of the most gifted players to wear the Rangers colours, but also one of the most frustrating. Cooper moved to Ibrox in June 1977 for £100,000 from his beloved Clydebank and was an immediate hit with the fans, who admired his exquisite left foot and mazy runs from the left wing. However, in spite of his amazing gifts, he was too often wasteful and attempted to beat one man too many when a simple pass would have been more advantageous.

Nevertheless, his was a glittering career; he collected 22 caps for Scotland as well as numerous domestic honours with Rangers. He won three League winner's medals, three Scottish Cups and no less than seven League Cups.

Cooper gained another Scottish Cup medal for

Motherwell, whom he joined in 1989 for £50,000 in the 1991 Final victory over Dundee United. His renaissance at Fir Park also prompted a recall to the Scotland team. But tragedy struck when, in 1995, he returned to Clydebank as a coach and, while making a film on coaching for youngsters, he suffered a severe brain haemorrhage and died the next day in a Glasgow hospital, aged just 39.

His untimely death united both sides of the sectarian barrier, with Celtic supporters joining thousands of football-loving Scots who were shocked by the brilliant winger's end. Cooper will always be remembered by Rangers fans who compared his left peg with that of another Ibrox legend, Jim Baxter – a comparison which would have left the winger extremely proud.

'*Davie Cooper is one of the greatest players Scotland has ever produced.*'
MAURICE JOHNSTON

31

1993-1997

Gordon Durie

PERSONAL FILE

Born: 6 December 1965
Birthplace: Paisley
Height: 6' 0"
Weight: 12st 0lb

LEAGUE RECORD

FROM-TO	CLUB	APPS	GOALS
1981-85	East Fife	81	26
1985-86	Hibernian	47	14
1986-92	Chelsea	123	51
1992-93	Tottenham	58	11
1993-97	Rangers	88	40
Total		397	142

RANGERS LEAGUE DEBUT

27 November 1993 v Partick Thistle

SCOTLAND DEBUT

11 November 1987 v Bulgaria

SCOTLAND HONOURS (TO 31 MAY 1997)

SEASON	CAPS
1987-88	1
1988-89	2
1989-90	4
1990-91	5
1991-92	9
1992-93	2
1993-94	4
1994-95	—
1995-96	4
1996-97	2
Total	33

DID YOU KNOW?

Gordon had a very unsatisfactory time at Spurs, which included a disagreement with manager Ossie Ardiles over a substitution.

Gordon Durie took the long way round finally to realise his dream of playing for Rangers. The striker began his career with East Fife, but made his name with Hibs before being sold to Chelsea. Durie flourished at Stamford Bridge and quickly became one of the English defenders' least favourite people with his fast, aggressive style. He also broke into the Scotland side and established himself as an important part of the international squad. That prompted Tottenham to launch a £2.5 million bid to take him across the capital.

Throughout his time at White Hart Lane there were rumours that Durie was moving to Rangers, and on several occasions the deal was claimed to have been completed. Finally, in 1993, Durie made a £1.5 million switch to Ibrox, making an immediate impact with 12 goals in 24 League games to help tie up the League Championship.

Injury problems restricted Durie's appearances the following season, but he quickly battled back and scored a tremendous hat-trick in the 1996 Scottish Cup Final win over Hearts.

Durie also had an outstanding European Championship in England the same year and was voted by many pundits as Scotland's top player. His 1996-97 season with Rangers, as they strode to their ninth consecutive title, was severely curtailed by injury, but despite a summer influx of new players, he seemed assured of a continued place in the squad should he return to full fitness.

1984-1997

Iain Durrant

PERSONAL FILE

Born: 29 October 1966
Birthplace: Glasgow
Height: 5' 8"
Weight: 9st 7lb

LEAGUE RECORD

FROM-TO	CLUB	APPS	GOALS
1984-97	Rangers	240	26
1994-95	Everton (loan)	5	—
	Total	245	26

RANGERS LEAGUE DEBUT

20 April 1985 v Morton

SCOTLAND DEBUT

9 September 1987 v Hungary

SCOTLAND HONOURS

SEASON	CAPS
1987-88	4
1988-89	1
1989-90	—
1990-91	—
1991-92	—
1992-93	4
1993-94	2
Total	11

STAR QUOTE

"My head was at Everton, but my heart will always be at Ibrox.'

Iain Durrant will go down in Scottish football history as one of the great unfulfilled talents. Durrant had all the ability to become the finest midfielder of his generation, but tragically that will never be realised. He signed for Rangers from the Glasgow United boys club with Scotland Youth honours already under his belt. And it wasn't long before he made his full debut as an 18-year-old.

He quickly became a favourite of the Rangers fans at the end of the second Jock Wallace era, which brought little success. His skill on the ball and fast attacking style made him stand out from the usual breed of hard-man Scottish midfielder.

When Graeme Souness took over at Ibrox in 1986, he quickly identified Durrant as his star asset and claimed he had as much natural talent as anyone he had seen. Two tremendous seasons followed, and it seemed certain Durrant was destined to be a Scotland regular at just 21. However, tragedy struck in October 1988, when a tackle from Aberdeen's Neil Simpson left him with serious knee ligament damage.

It seemed at one stage that his career could be over, and he spent almost two seasons on the sidelines before returning to fitness. He slowly made his way back into first-team contention and seemed to rekindle his old sparkle for the 1992-93 season. Durrant was in outstanding form and hit crucial goals as Rangers came within a whisker of making the European Cup Final.

However that form didn't last, and Durrant was almost sold to Everton in 1995 after a loan spell at Goodison. He returned to Ibrox and made fleeting appearances in the first team, but has yet to recclaim a regular spot.

33

1993-1994

Duncan Ferguson

PERSONAL FILE

Born: 27 December 1971
Birthplace: Stirling
Height: 6' 3"
Weight: 13st 8lb

LEAGUE RECORD

FROM-TO	CLUB	APPS	GOALS
1990-93	Dundee Utd	77	28
1993-94	Rangers	14	2
1994-97	Everton	92	27
Total		183	57

RANGERS LEAGUE DEBUT

21 August 1993 v Celtic

SCOTLAND DEBUT

17 May 1992 v USA

SCOTLAND HONOURS
(TO 31 MAY 1997)

SEASON	CAPS
1991-92	3
1992-93	1
1993-94	—
1994-95	1
1995-96	—
1996-97	2
Total	7

STAR QUOTE

'It's important to get Duncan out of Scotland...he's a marked man there.'
JOE ROYLE

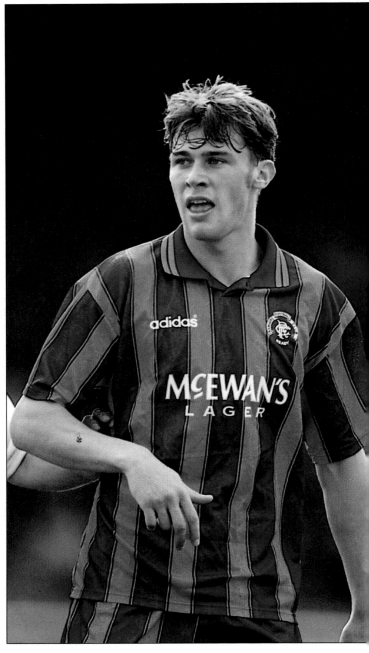

Scottish football is littered with players who have courted controversy and 'Big Dunc' is the latest of that long line. The six-foot-three-inch striker from Stirling has seen more highs, lows, hatred and hero-worship than most players can dream of. Ferguson was snapped up on schoolboy forms by Dundee United, and it wasn't long before he made his mark in the first team. Nine appearances and one goal in the 1990-91 season soon had people talking about the lanky kid at Tannadice with great skill in his feet as well as his head.

The following season he produced 15 goals, and 12 the next, as it became clear he was the new great Scottish hope. But off the park he couldn't stay out of trouble, and ended up with a string of convictions, for scuffles in a bar and one at a taxi rank. However, the dark side of Ferguson didn't deter Rangers and in the summer of 1993, Walter Smith shocked British football when he paid out £4 million for his signature.

Unfortunately, it seemed he couldn't cope with all the hype and pressure, and made just 14 League appearances in just over a season at Ibrox. The most infamous incident was against Raith Rovers when he headbutted Jock McStay: Ferguson was sentenced to six months in Glasgow's Barlinnie prison, of which he served three. A move to Everton seemed the best solution for all, and he quickly became a cult hero to the blue half of Merseyside. A potential Rangers all-time great had fulfilled his promise in a different shade of blue.

1988-1997

Ian Ferguson

PERSONAL FILE

Born: 15 March 1967
Birthplace: Glasgow
Height: 5' 10"
Weight: 10st 11lb

LEAGUE RECORD

FROM-TO	CLUB	APPS	GOALS
1984-86	Clyde	26	4
1986-88	St Mirren	57	10
1988-97	Rangers	211	22
Total		294	36

RANGERS LEAGUE DEBUT

27 February 1988 v Dundee United

SCOTLAND DEBUT

22 December 1988 v Italy

SCOTLAND HONOURS (TO 31 MAY 1997)

SEASON	CAPS
1988-89	3
1989-90	—
1990-91	—
1991-92	—
1992-93	2
1993-94	3
1994-95	—
1995-96	—
1996-97	1
Total	9

DID YOU KNOW?

A rare misdemeanour which brought Ian a ban was a clash with future team-mate Petric in 1993-94.

Hard-working, aggressive and a player instilled with the traditional Rangers 'never say die' spirit, Ferguson was the first player to be transferred for £1 million between two Scottish clubs when he moved to Ibrox from St Mirren in 1988. He began his career at Clyde and spent three seasons there before moving to Love Street. It was with St Mirren in the Premier League that his talents became recognised and he secured his place in their history with the winning goal in the 1987 Scottish Cup Final.

That feat helped secure his move to Rangers, the team he had supported as a boy growing up in the shadow of Parkhead in Glasgow's East End. Ferguson quickly claimed his spot in the Gers midfield, adding the aggression and passing ability lost when Graeme Souness hung up his boots. And he helped the club to a classic League Cup triumph over Aberdeen with an overhead kick goal in a 3–2 Hampden win. Ferguson also staked his claim on the international scene and picked up caps, without ever being a Scotland regular.

Sections of the Rangers fans had doubts about his ability, but none of them questioned his passion for the light blue jersey. And in an era of multi-million-pound foreign superstars there are few other players they would rather have when the chips are down.

Tom Forsyth

PERSONAL FILE

Born: 23 January 1949
Birthplace: Glasgow
Height: 5' 11"
Weight: 12st 2lb

LEAGUE RECORD

FROM-TO	CLUB	APPS	GOALS
1967-72	Motherwell	n/k	n/k
1972-82	Rangers	220	1
Total		220	1

RANGERS LEAGUE DEBUT

14 October 1972 v Motherwell

SCOTLAND DEBUT

9 June 1971 v Denmark

SCOTLAND HONOURS

SEASON	CAPS
1970-71	1
1971-72	—
1972-73	—
1973-74	1
1974-75	—
1975-76	4
1976-77	8
1977-78	8
Total	22

DID YOU KNOW?
Forsyth had only played a single Under-23 game before being called up for his first full Scotland international in 1971.

An uncompromising, ball-winning midfielder, Tom Forsyth rejoiced in the nickname of 'Jaws' from his Ibrox team-mates. Yet to damn him as a purely destructive player is to deny the talents that won him not only 22 full caps for his country but also a place in an impressive Rangers side. Three League titles, four Scottish FA Cups and a League Cup would also be added to his personal trophy cabinet during his Ibrox stay.

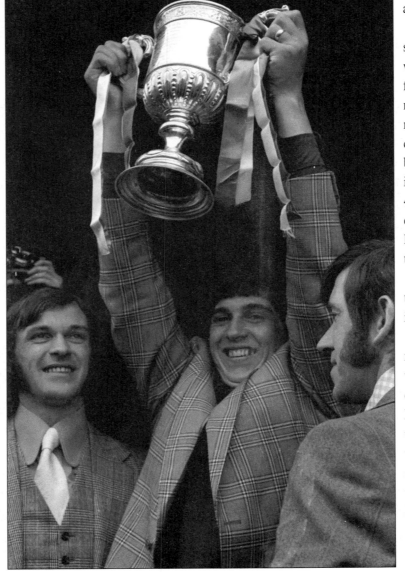

Five seasons at Motherwell ended with a £40,000 move to Ibrox sanctioned in October 1972 by new team manager Jock Wallace. Ironically, his first appearance in the blue and white came at Fir Park against his former club, where he wore the Number 8 shirt and came away with a win. He made 21 appearances in his first season – Rangers finishing second – and though the following season was curtailed half-way through by injury he returned to help the Gers to their first League title for 11 years in 1974-75, playing 30 times and registering his first League goal against Morton in October.

Scotland caps had been as scarce as his net-busting, a debut while still at Motherwell being followed by just one more in the next four seasons. But as he made his mark at Ibrox the chances started coming, helped by another Championship season in 1975-76. Now in the Number 4 shirt, denoting a more defensive role, he remained a linchpin of Jock Wallace's side that took a third title in 1978.

But John Greig's accession to the throne saw 'Jaws' discarded in favour of fresher fish and by 1980-81, his appearances were more frequently as sub. Injuries were taking their toll and he officially retired in March 1982. Dunfermline appointed him as their manager six months later, while his next stop in the close season of 1985 saw him back with first club Motherwell as assistant manager.

1995-1997

Paul Gascoigne

PERSONAL FILE

Born: 27 May 1967
Birthplace: Gateshead
Height: 5' 10"
Weight: 11st 7lb

LEAGUE RECORD

FROM-TO	CLUB	APPS	GOALS
1984-88	Newcastle Utd	92	21
1988-93	Tottenham H	92	19
1993-95	Lazio	41	6
1995-97	Rangers	53	27
Total		278	73

RANGERS LEAGUE DEBUT

9 September 1995 v Raith Rovers

ENGLAND DEBUT

14 September 1988 v Denmark

ENGLAND HONOURS
(TO 31 MAY 1997)

SEASON	CAPS
1988-89	5
1989-90	12
1990-91	3
1991-92	—
1992-93	7
1993-94	2
1994-95	3
1995-96	11
1996-97	5
Total	48

STAR QUOTE

'I just want to get on with enjoying football again, and I know I'll do that at Rangers.'

When Rangers brought Paul Gascoigne back from Italy in the summer of 1995 they were not only acquiring a player of immense talent, but a man whose whole career had been dogged by controversy. Rangers manager Walter Smith had no compunction about paying the £4.5 million asking price that Lazio of Rome wanted for the former Newcastle United and Tottenham Hotspur midfielder, as he sought to continue his club's rule at home and enhance their stature in European competitions.

Gazza, however, has proved a mixed blessing for Smith and has sorely tested his patience, as he has with previous managers like Bobby Robson and Terry Venables. But there can be no doubt that, from Italia '90 onwards, he was probably England's only real world-class player.

A player of sublime skill and vision, Gascoigne is also capable of crass stupidity and toe-curling childishness. His ability, in the twinkling of an eye, to turn a game – the superb goal in the England-Scotland game in the 1996 European Championships, for example – is often put in the shade by stupid tantrums and thoughtless behaviour.

His transfer to Lazio was delayed by a year when, following a reckless challenge on Nottingham Forest's Gary Charles in the 1991 FA Cup Final for Tottenham, he seriously damaged his knee.

Nevertheless, his contribution to Rangers is best summed up by their performances when he is missing, either through suspension or injury. Gascoigne, during one particularly self-indulgent spell, incurred the wrath of officials in Scotland to such an extent that his tenure at Ibrox in 1996 looked set to be brief. But he recovered to help Gers to the League and Cup Double and was voted Scotland's Player of the Year.

Smith has made Gascoigne the conduit through which Rangers' most creative and dangerous moves pass. The Geordie's marvellous close control, his ability to run at defenders and, probably almost as crucial, his vision and quickness of thought have often snatched victory from the jaws of defeat, as Smith's team have continued their amazing dominance north of the border.

Though transfer speculation abounded at Lazio, Rangers were the only club to put in a firm offer for Gazza.

Andy Goram

PERSONAL FILE

Born: 13 April 1964
Birthplace: Bury
Height: 5' 11"
Weight: 11st 6lb

LEAGUE RECORD

FROM-TO	CLUB	APPS	GOALS
1981-87	Oldham Ath	195	—
1987-91	Hibernian	138	1
1991-97	Rangers	160	—
Total		493	1

RANGERS LEAGUE DEBUT

10 August 1991 v St Johnstone

SCOTLAND DEBUT

16 October 1985 v East Germany

SCOTLAND HONOURS

SEASON	CAPS
1985-86	3
1986-87	1
1987-88	—
1988-89	2
1989-90	3
1990-91	6
1991-92	8
1992-93	5
1993-94	1
1994-95	4
1995-96	6
1996-97	3
Total	42

STAR QUOTE

'I hope to be here so long they have to kick me out!'

Commanding keeper Andy Goram has been a key figure in goal for Rangers as their dominance of the Scottish scene has continued in the 1990s. The Bury-born shot-stopper began his career with nearby Oldham Athletic for whom he signed in 1981 as a teenager and stayed until his love affair with Scotland began at Hibernian in 1987. Goram built a formidable reputation in the Edinburgh side during the course of four seasons – he even scored a goal in his first term at Easter Road. And it was no surprise when his reliability and alertness in the penalty area were recognised at Ibrox and he was persuaded to join Rangers in 1991.

Already a Scotland international from his days in Lancashire, Goram's performances in Walter Smith's team have brought him universal praise and respect. Although far from tall by goalkeeping standards at five foot 11 inches, his safe handling and speed around the box have broken the hearts of many a striker.

Goram is also a master of the one-on-one situation. Such is his reputation that, like Peter Shilton and Neville Southall, forwards are regularly thwarted by his fearless and explosive bursts from the goal-line to block or smother shots.

He has amassed a tally of six Championship winner's medals, three Scottish Cup medals and two League Cup medals during his amazingly successful stint with the club. But Goram's talents are not restricted to football, for he is also a cricket international and has represented Scotland on many occasions.

Goram has admitted an alternate profession could have been a labourer if it had not been for his sporting prowess.

1987-1997

Richard Gough

PERSONAL FILE

Born: 5 April 1962
Birthplace: Stockholm
Height: 5' 9"
Weight: 11st 2lb

LEAGUE RECORD

FROM-TO	CLUB	APPS	GOALS
1980-86	Dundee Utd	165	23
1986-87	Tottenham H	49	2
1987-97	Rangers	294	25
Total		508	50

RANGERS LEAGUE DEBUT

10 October 1987 v Dundee Utd

SCOTLAND DEBUT

30 March 1983 v Switzerland

SCOTLAND HONOURS

SEASON	CAPS
1982-83	7
1983-84	7
1984-85	3
1985-86	9
1986-86	7
1987-88	5
1988-89	5
1989-90	7
1990-91	2
1991-92	7
1992-93	2
Total	61

STAR QUOTE

'We should be looking to win every home game by 4-0 and 5-0, because we have better players.'

After being turned down by the club as a teenager, Richard Gough returned to Rangers in a £1 million deal to become one of the most successful captains in the club's long and proud history.

Gough was born in Stockholm in 1962 of a Swedish mother and a Scottish father who, fortunately for Rangers, was an ardent Ibrox follower. After spending much of his childhood in South Africa, Gough had a trial for Rangers, but was not considered good enough and was picked up by Dundee United's manager Jim McLean.

He stayed at Tannadice for six years and, despite overtures from Ibrox, Gough was persuaded to move south to become captain of Tottenham Hotspur for a fee of £500,000. He led them to the 1987 FA Cup Final at Wembley, which Spurs surprisingly lost 3-2 to Coventry City.

But by December that year, Gough was back where he always wanted to be, at Ibrox, after new player-manager Graeme Souness had paid £1.1 million for his services. Gough quickly formed a central defensive partnership with Terry Butcher, and his brave heading ability and incisive tackling paved the way for Rangers' future success.

Gough's Scotland career – he won 61 caps for his adopted country – was cut short by public disagreement with then national coach Andy Roxburgh, who elected not to choose him, a policy continued under present boss Craig Brown.

But if Gough's international appearances dried up, his appetite for silverware certainly did not. With Rangers' record-equalling nine-in-a-row League Championship success in 1997, the elegant defender accrued his 18th major honour while at Ibrox. After levelling with Celtic's incredible tally, Gough bowed out of Govan to parade his footballing talents further west with Kansas City in the US.

His father Charles was a professional with Charlton Athletic in the 1960s.

1961-1978

John Greig

PERSONAL FILE

Born: 11 September 1942
Birthplace: Edinburgh
Height: 5' 10"
Weight: 11st 2lb

LEAGUE RECORD

FROM-TO	CLUB	APPS	GOALS
1961-78	Rangers	496	87

RANGERS LEAGUE DEBUT

18 November 1961 v Falkirk

SCOTLAND DEBUT

11 April 1964 v England

SCOTLAND HONOURS

SEASON	CAPS
1963-64	2
1964-65	7
1965-66	9
1966-67	3
1967-68	4
1968-69	8
1969-70	5
1970-71	5
1971-72	—
1972-73	—
1973-74	—
1974-75	—
1975-76	1
Total	44

DID YOU KNOW?
A crowd of 65,000 at Greig's testimonial saw Rangers beat a Scotland XI 5-0 in 1978.

The much over-used word 'great', so often applied to the undeserving, not only applies to John Greig but still fails to do full justice to this legendary Ibrox giant. Greig, now honoured with an MBE for services to football, represented Rangers and Scotland with great distinction for 18 years, winning five League Championship, six Scottish Cup and four League Cup medals. He was involved in winning the Treble on three occasions – the only Scot to have done so – in 1964, 1976 and 1978. But mere statistics do him an injustice, for it was his leadership qualities that stood him apart from his peers and will forever endear him to all Scottish supporters.

Although Greig was not the most gifted of footballers, his potential was spotted by Rangers' manager Scot Symon while playing for Edina Hearts in his native Edinburgh in 1961. Symon converted him from an inside-forward to a wing-half and, with Ronnie McKinnon and Jim Baxter, he formed the axis on which Symon was to build his great 1960s team.

Greig, twice voted Scotland's Player of the Year, skippered Rangers to their European Cup Winners' Cup success in 1972 and, six years later, hung up his boots for good to bring his pragmatism and integrity to the job of managing the club. In spite of enjoying Scottish Cup and League Cup successes and introducing Rangers fans to the likes of Ally McCoist, Iain Durrant and Derek Ferguson, Greig's failure to land the League title forced him to resign in November 1983.

He left his beloved Ibrox for seven years before returning in 1990 to take up a post in public relations, a role he still serves with distinction – you would expect no less from this one-club gentleman.

1990-1995 & 1997

Mark Hateley

PERSONAL FILE

Born: 7 November 1961
Birthplace: Liverpool
Height: 6' 1"
Weight: 11st 7lb

LEAGUE RECORD

FROM-TO	CLUB	APPS	GOALS
1978-83	Coventry C	93	25
1983-84	Portsmouth	38	22
1984-87	AC Milan	66	17
1987-90	Monaco	59	22
1990-95	Rangers	165	85
1995-96	QPR	27	3
1997	Leeds Utd	6	—
1997	Rangers	4	1
Total		458	175

RANGERS LEAGUE DEBUT
25 August 1990 v Dunfermline

ENGLAND DEBUT
2 June 1984 v USSR

ENGLAND HONOURS

SEASON	CAPS
1983-84	4
1984-85	8
1985-86	9
1986-87	3
1987-88	7
1988-89	—
1989-90	—
1990-91	—
1991-92	1
Total	32

DID YOU KNOW?
Mark's best Rangers season, 1993-94, saw him the Premier League's top scorer and Scottish Player of the Year.

Nicknamed 'Attila' by the Italian media – for both his name and his flowing black hair when bearing down on apprehensive defences – Mark Hateley enjoyed great success both internationally and domestically as a menacing striker.

Born in Liverpool in 1961, Hateley had football in his blood as his father, Tony, was a much-travelled centre-forward for clubs including Liverpool and Aston Villa. Hateley junior began his professional career with Coventry in 1978, before moving to Portsmouth five years later. His star was in the ascendancy when, in 1984, he scored a memorable goal in England's 2-0 victory in the Maracana Stadium in Rio De Janeiro and he moved to AC Milan for £900,000.

His wanderlust took him to Monaco four years later for £1 million, where he was in the Principality's Championship-winning side. Graeme Souness, who knew all about Hateley's qualities from his time in Italy, paid another million for him in 1990.

Hateley repaid part of the fee in the final match of the 1990-91 season, when he scored both goals in the 2-0 victory over Aberdeen at Ibrox in front of over 37,000 fans: it deprived the Dons, who needed only a point to secure the title, of the Championship.

He was capped 32 times for his country and, in many people's opinion, it should have been more during his spell with Rangers for whom he scored 136 goals in 241 matches. After winning five Championship titles with Rangers he moved in 1995 to Queens Park Rangers, but rejoined the club for a brief spell at a cost of £400,000 in 1997 before taking a first step into management with Hull City.

Willie Henderson

PERSONAL FILE

Born:	24 January 1944
Birthplace:	Glasgow
Height:	5' 4"
Weight:	10st 3lb

LEAGUE RECORD

FROM-TO	CLUB	APPS	GOALS
1961-72	Rangers	276	36
1972-74	Sheffield Wed	48	5
1974-77	Hong Kong Rangers	n/k	n/k
1978-79	Airdrie	n/k	n/k
Total		324	41

RANGERS LEAGUE DEBUT

28 March 1961 v Clyde

SCOTLAND DEBUT

20 October 1962 v Wales

SCOTLAND HONOURS

SEASON	CAPS
1962-63	7
1963-64	5
1964-65	4
1965-66	5
1966-67	2
1967-68	1
1968-69	3
1969-70	1
1970-71	1
Total	29

DID YOU KNOW?
Only Denis Law in modern times has played for Scotland at a younger age than Willie Henderson.

By anyone's yardstick, winger Willie Henderson was what you would call a child prodigy. His path from Airdrie Schools to Rangers via Edinburgh Athletic won him Scottish Schoolboy honours: he was in the first team at 17 and a year later had received full honours for his country.

Twenty-eight more caps would follow in the next nine seasons, but would tail off as he found that early supernova success hard to sustain. At club level, though, he was unstoppable. Operating in tandem with Davie Wilson on the left wing, he fed strikers Millar and Brand with umpteen goalscoring opportunities.

At just over five foot four, Henderson's centre of gravity was low and this, combined with speed and enviable ball control, would find him twisting full-backs inside and out before beating them on the touchline side. The Ibrox crowd understandably adopted him as a hero and he played to the gallery with aplomb. His arrival on the scene displaced Alex Scott, another international-class raider, who promptly moved on to Everton.

Though entertaining for fans, a two-season spell south of the border at Hillsborough (where he moved in 1972 after a brief spell in South Africa), was spent in the Second Division, and he moved on to Hong Kong for a three year spell, ironically with the local Rangers club. He also captained the Hong Kong national side before moving back for a swansong with Airdrie.

Injury problems conspired to blunt Henderson's impact in later years: he was also forced to take up wearing contact lenses.

But all the full-backs who faced him were left with was a view of the cleanest pair of heels in the Scottish League.

1963-1982

Colin Jackson

PERSONAL FILE

Born: 8 October 1946
Birthplace: London
Height: 6' 0"
Weight: 12st 5lb

LEAGUE RECORD

FROM-TO	CLUB	APPS	GOALS
1963-82	Rangers	343	23

RANGERS LEAGUE DEBUT

1 January 1966 v Partick Thistle

SCOTLAND DEBUT

16 April 1975 v Sweden

SCOTLAND HONOURS

SEASON	CAPS
1974-75	3
1975-76	5
Total	8

DID YOU KNOW?
After retiring from football, Jackson became a partner in an East Kilbride printing firm.

There are few players who have given so much to one club as Colin Jackson, who graced the Rangers staff for 20 seasons. He had the ability to read the game from his defensive berth at centre-half and established himself as being a difficult defender to beat due to his immaculate positional sense.

London-born Jackson remains one of the few players to have been born outside Scotland and still represent them at international level, having been capped eight times. He moved to Rangers in 1963 from Sunnybank Athletic, a small team from Aberdeen and stayed with the club until 1982.

Rangers' 1972 European Cup Winners' Cup win will always rankle with this popular giant of a centre-half. Injury prevented Jackson from taking the field in Barcelona, and he had to watch a young Derek Johnstone play in his place after the 3–2 defeat of Moscow Dynamo. However, despite this setback, Jackson still won his fair share of medals in a Rangers career which saw him play over 500 games for the Ibrox side.

An uncompromising stopper who was hard in the tackle and simple in his distribution of the ball, he and John Greig were the backbone of the team with which Jock Wallace won two Trebles in three years.

He only ever played for Rangers, the team he supported as a boy, and retired at 35 after a crushing 4–1 Scottish Cup Final defeat to Aberdeen. Jackson retains his close connections with Ibrox today by assisting Rangers' commercial side as a matchday host.

1967- 1982

Sandy Jardine

DID YOU KNOW?
Jardine was the first Scottish-born player to record over 1,000 first-class matches.

William Pullar 'Sandy' Jardine was a manager's dream: skilful, elegant, scrupulously fair and, above all, loyal. Edinburgh-born Jardine was signed by Rangers' fourth manager, David White, as a precociously talented 18-year-old at the start of 1967. He arrived at a shell-shocked Ibrox just one week after Rangers were knocked out of the Scottish Cup First Round by Berwick – one of the greatest upsets in Scottish footballing history.

But his debut, against his boyhood club Hearts, was more auspicious, for Rangers thumped the Jambos 5-1. Little did the promising teenager realise that 15 years later he would be turning out in the famous maroon shirts after his remarkable career with the Glasgow giants was over.

Jardine was the model professional whose versatility was a byword among his peers. Although at one time or another he played in all the defensive positions – even up front – it was at right-back that he excelled. He made 38 appearances for Scotland and indeed he was so established at this level, that Celtic's superb Danny McGrain was forced to move to left-back for international matches!

Strong, cultured and extremely fast at either going forward, or returning for the covering tackle, Jardine was in the Rangers side that lost 1-0 to Bayern Munich in the European Cup Winners' Cup in 1967. But five years later, he was able to enjoy the sweet taste of success as Rangers lifted the trophy after beating Moscow Dynamo 3-2 in Barcelona.

Jardine was also included in the Scotland World Cup squad for the 1974 and 1978 Finals, in Germany and Argentina respectively. So well was he thought of, that he received the sportswriters' Player of the Year award on two occasions.

His career with Rangers ended after the 1982 Scottish Cup Final on a celebratory note after his side triumphed over Aberdeen 4-1. Jardine had made nearly 700 appearances in the famous blue and white.

Still superbly fit, even at 33, Jardine joined his home-town club, Hearts, and went on to manage them.

1964-1972 & 1980-1982

Willie Johnston

PERSONAL FILE

Born: 19 December 1946
Birthplace: Glasgow
Height: 5' 7"
Weight: 11st 0lb

LEAGUE RECORD

FROM-TO	CLUB	APPS	GOALS
1964-72	Rangers	211	89
1972-79	West Brom	207	18
1979-80	Vancouver W'caps	41	3
1979-80	Birmingham C (loan)	15	—
1980-82	Rangers	35	2
1982-85	Hearts	n/k	n/k
Total		509	112

RANGERS LEAGUE DEBUT

6 October 1964 v St Johnstone

SCOTLAND DEBUT

13 October 1965 v Poland

SCOTLAND HONOURS

SEASON	CAPS
1965-66	4
1966-67	—
1967-68	2
1968-69	1
1969-70	1
1970-71	1
1971-72	—
1972-73	—
1973-74	—
1974-75	—
1975-76	—
1976-77	7
1977-78	6
Total	22

DID YOU KNOW?

In the 1968-69 season, Willie Johnston scored eight goals at Parkhead – though three were against Aberdeen in a Cup Semi-Final.

Willie Johnston's career was the proverbial curate's egg as a player with Rangers: he proved to be one of the best postwar goalscoring wingers but, sadly, boasted one of the most dreadful disciplinary records imaginable.

During the course of a long career of highs and lows, the fiery Glaswegian was ordered off no less than 20 times and turned managers' hair grey at both domestic and international levels.

Johnston's was a precocious talent that first blossomed for his junior club in Fife before signing for Rangers at the age of 17. He began playing inside Scotland left-winger Davie Wilson, but his talent soon made the wide berth his own. His lightning-quick, dazzling runs down the left thrilled hundreds of thousands of fans all over the world. But when the other side of the Johnston coin flipped, there was normally only one outcome.

Willie's finest moment was in scoring two of Rangers goals in their 3-2 victory over Moscow Dynamo to win the European Cup Winners' Cup in Barcelona in 1972. His low point came in Argentina during the 1978 World Cup when he was sent home after failing a drug test. He was suspended by FIFA and his great talents were lost to international football.

Rangers sold him to West Bromwich Albion for £135,000 in December 1972, after he had served a nine-week suspension for being sent off in a clash with Partick Thistle. Johnston served the Baggies well before joining Vancouver Whitecaps in 1979 and then returning to Rangers, under the long-suffering John Greig, one year later. But he was sent off, yet again, within weeks of his arrival. He ended his career with Hearts, retiring within reach of his 40th birthday.

1970-1983 & 1985-1986

PERSONAL FILE

Born: 4 November 1953
Birthplace: Dundee
Height: 6' 0"
Weight: 13st 2lb

LEAGUE RECORD

FROM-TO	CLUB	APPS	GOALS
1970-83	Rangers	356	121
1983-85	Chelsea	4	—
1983	Dundee Utd (loan)	4	—
1985-86	Rangers	19	1
Total		383	122

RANGERS LEAGUE DEBUT

19 September 1970 v Cowdenbeath

SCOTLAND DEBUT

12 May 1973 v Wales

SCOTLAND HONOURS

SEASON	CAPS
1972-73	5
1973-74	—
1974-75	2
1975-76	3
1976-77	—
1977-78	3
1978-79	—
1979-80	1
Total	14

DID YOU KNOW?
Johnstone's fifth and last Scottish Cup medal came when he replaced Colin McAdam for the 1981 Final replay.

Derek Johnstone

Few can say that they have played in defence, midfield and as centre-forward for both club and country. Derek Johnstone was one of the rare breed of players who not only achieved this but also proved themselves to be skilled in each position. Tall and well-built, Johnstone used his physical prowess to score over 200 goals in his career despite the fact that he favoured the centre-half position.

He moved to Rangers in 1968, having come from the youth side of home-town club Dundee United. He turned pro in July 1970 and made his first-team debut in September against Cowdenbeath. He won a permanent place in fans' affections just one month later by scoring the only goal in the League Cup Final. Not only was this Johnstone's first Cup Final – he was not even 17 at the time – it was also his first Old Firm match. Rangers and Celtic followers alike never forgot him after that.

With such a dramatic start to his career, Johnstone always seemed destined for greatness, and his record for his club lived up to this expectation. Not only did he establish himself in the Rangers squad of the 1970s which seemed to win titles at will, he was instrumental to their success. The sheer quantity of his honours was impressive enough, not to mention the fact that he scored crucial goals in several Finals and, as previously mentioned, helped his side win trophies while playing in all three positions.

Johnstone left the club in 1983 and moved first to Chelsea and then briefly on to his first love, Dundee United, before returning to Rangers in January 1985. He left the club a year later to manage Partick and currently reviews the Glasgow scene as a respected commentator for Radio Clyde.

'It didn't matter what I did...I was the lad that
scored the goal against Celtic to win the Cup.'

1994-1997

Brian Laudrup

PERSONAL FILE

Born: 22 February 1969
Birthplace: Vienna
Height: 6' 0"
Weight: 13st 2lb

LEAGUE RECORD

FROM-TO	CLUB	APPS	GOALS
1986-89	Brondby	n/k	n/k
1989-90	Bayer Uerdingen	n/k	n/k
1990-92	Bayern Munich	n/k	n/k
1992-94	Fiorentina	n/k	n/k
1994	AC Milan (loan)	9	1
1994-97	Rangers	88	28
Total		97	29

RANGERS LEAGUE DEBUT

13 August 1994 v Motherwell

DENMARK HONOURS

Had been capped 63 times by his country by the start of 1996-97

STAR QUOTE
'Even opponents admire him greatly...he conducts himself well on and off the park.'
WALTER SMITH

52

I n Danish international Brian Laudrup, Rangers have a player who is truly world class and who has few peers either domestically or internationally. Put simply, he is adored by the Ibrox faithful and admired by the opposition. Rangers manager Walter Smith brought Laudrup from Fiorentina in 1994 for a price in excess of £3 million. But in the present climate of inflated transfer fees, Smith's capture has proved to have been a shrewd and fiscally canny one.

Born in Vienna in February 1969, Laudrup was made to play the beautiful game. His father, Finn, was capped 21 times for Denmark, while older brother Michael has played both for Barcelona and Juventus with great distinction. Indeed, Michael was in the Denmark side that surprisingly lifted the European Championships in 1992.

Laudrup began his career with Brondby, before moving to Germany for £650,000 to join Bayer Uerdingen. But his talents soon became apparent and Bayern Munich paid £2 million for him. Laudrup's move to Fiorentina was followed by a loan spell at AC Milan, but he never enjoyed the style of football there, and it is under Smith's benevolent tactics that his true potential as a playmaker has blossomed.

For a player with such exquisite ball skills and breathtaking pace, Laudrup is a big man, standing at six foot and weighing over 13 stone. He soon established himself as a favourite at Rangers in his first season (1994-95) and was voted the Player of the Year by sportswriters and players at the end of that campaign, after scoring 13 times in less than 40 matches.

His brilliance shone through to a British television audience in Rangers' emphatic 5-1 Scottish Cup success over hapless Hearts in 1996, when he scored twice himself and had a hand in the other three which striker Gordon Durie bagged. Laudrup is a superb individual talent, but one whose unselfishness has marked him out as a rare talent indeed.

Alex McDonald

PERSONAL FILE

Born: 17 March 1948
Birthplace: Glasgow
Height: 5' 6"
Weight: 10st 10lb

LEAGUE RECORD

FROM-TO	CLUB	APPS	GOALS
1966-68	St Johnstone	n/k	n/k
1968-80	Rangers	306	51
1980-85	Hearts	n/k	n/k
Total		306	51

RANGERS LEAGUE DEBUT
23 November 1968 v Clyde

SCOTLAND DEBUT
7 April 1976 v Switzerland

SCOTLAND HONOURS

SEASON	CAPS
1975-76	1
Total	1

DID YOU KNOW?
Having joined Hearts as player-manager five years earlier, Alex McDonald was voted Scotland's Manager of the Year in 1986.

Alexander McDonald was a tough little battler, playing on the left side of midfield, who perhaps was overshadowed and under-praised in the successful Rangers sides of the 1970s. Manager Davie White lured McDonald away from St Johnstone in 1968 for a fee of £50,000 and, in a long and distinguished career at Ibrox, 'Doddie' went on to make 500 appearances for the club.

Luckily for White and Rangers, McDonald was a Glaswegian and blue through and through, but it took a while for his attributes to be appreciated by the supporters. Yet once they took to him, he became a firm favourite. McDonald won 12 major honours in his 13 years at Govan, and was a member of the side that won the European Cup Winners' Cup in 1972.

McDonald scored a surprisingly large number of goals for a ball-winner, 92 in total, including his header that clinched the 1-0 victory over Celtic in the 1976 League Cup Final. That was the same year Rangers completed the Treble in Scotland.

McDonald left Ibrox in 1981 to become player-manager of Hearts, where he enjoyed great success and acclaim

. Ironically for a true 'blue nose', it was McDonald's current charges Airdrie who gave Celtic their only piece of silverware in the 1990s – the Scottish Cup in 1995, courtesy of a Pierre Van Hooijdonk goal.

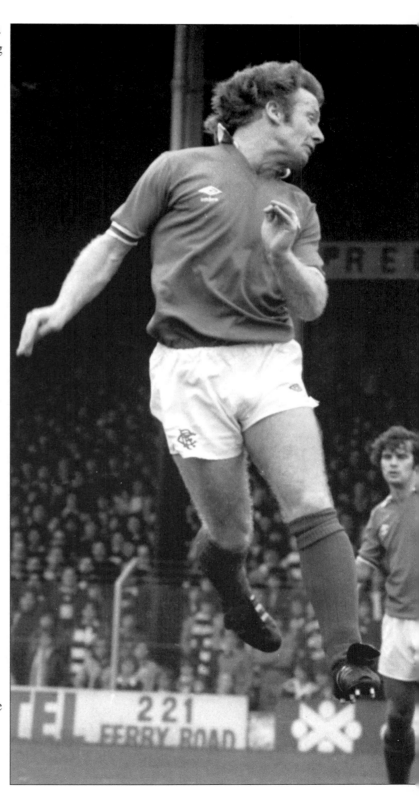

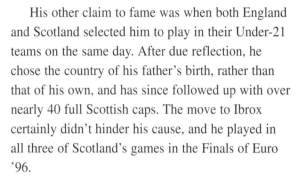

Stuart McCall

PERSONAL FILE

Born: 10 June 1964
Birthplace: Leeds
Height: 5' 6"
Weight: 10st 1lb

LEAGUE RECORD

FROM-TO	CLUB	APPS	GOALS
1982-88	Bradford C	238	37
1988-91	Everton	103	6
1991-97	Rangers	164	14
Total		505	57

RANGERS LEAGUE DEBUT

17 August 1991 v Hearts

SCOTLAND DEBUT

28 March 1990 v Argentina

SCOTLAND HONOURS
(TO 31 MAY 1997)

SEASON	CAPS
1989-90	8
1990-91	3
1991-92	9
1992-93	3
1993-94	4
1994-95	3
1995-96	7
1996-97	2
Total	39

STAR QUOTE

'The amount of running I do means I'm not going to play in midfield forever.'

Red-haired midfield dynamo Stuart McCall was transferred to Rangers in August 1991 from Everton after beginning his career with Bradford City. He'd achieved greatest fame for two reasons, most recently for participating in 1989's all-Merseyside FA Cup Final, when Liverpool beat Everton 3-2 after extra time and in which both he and opponent Ian Rush became the first substitutes to score twice in the history of the fixture.

His other claim to fame was when both England and Scotland selected him to play in their Under-21 teams on the same day. After due reflection, he chose the country of his father's birth, rather than that of his own, and has since followed up with over nearly 40 full Scottish caps. The move to Ibrox certainly didn't hinder his cause, and he played in all three of Scotland's games in the Finals of Euro '96.

His all-purpose abilities, both in tigerish ball-winning and intelligently supplying his team-mates, made McCall the ideal midfield counterpart to playmaker Paul Gascoigne at club level, just as he provided Gary McAllister with the same support in Scotland's darker blue. His all-action, non-stop effort could, however, be complemented with a greater strike rate: his 1989 feat at Wembley represents some two-thirds of his average League total for a season since joining Rangers.

Now well into his early thirties, Stuart McCall is not only one of Rangers' elder statesmen but an increasing rarity – a Scot. Unfortunately, the 1996-97 season was one in which he was sidelined by a succession of injuries, playing only the first seven League games and a handful of cup ties before becoming a resident on the treatment table. He would need to overcome such problems to make a continued mark in his seventh season at Ibrox and play a part as Rangers went for an historic 'ten in a row'.

Peter McCloy

PERSONAL FILE

Born: 16 November 1946
Birthplace: Girvan, Ayrshire
Height: 6' 4"
Weight: 14st 3lb

LEAGUE RECORD

FROM-TO	CLUB	APPS	GOALS
1964-70	Motherwell	n/k	n/k
1970-86	Rangers	351	—
Total		351	—

RANGERS LEAGUE DEBUT

14 March 1970 v Dunfermline

SCOTLAND DEBUT

12 May 1973 v Wales

SCOTLAND HONOURS

SEASON	CAPS
1972-73	4
Total	4

DID YOU KNOW?

As well as his Scottish football caps, McCloy has represented his country in amateur golf.

Every great team needs a great goalkeeper. The all-conquering Liverpool of the 1970s and 1980s had Ray Clemence and then Bruce Grobbelaar, and legendary Nottingham Forest manager Brian Clough brought in Peter Shilton to ensure success. The current Rangers boss Walter Smith has Andy Goram as his anchor to steady the ship when it becomes choppy at the back.

In the same way, the Rangers manager of the time, Willie Waddell, signed his 'Girvan Lighthouse', Peter McCloy, to add consistency to his brilliant team in 1970. McCloy earned his nickname because, at six foot four inches, he was probably one of the tallest keepers in the game, and because he hailed from Girvan on the coast of Ayrshire. McCloy's father had also played between the sticks with St Mirren, and Peter himself had begun his career at Fir Park with Motherwell.

The big man had an inauspicious start when Rangers went down 2-1 to Dunfermline in his first match, but his size and safe handling ensured he would be a fixture in goal for over a decade. McCloy was in the Rangers side at Barcelona, where they beat Moscow Dynamo 3-2 in 1972's Cup Winners' Cup Final. In fact, he helped create Rangers' third goal with a long clearance that eluded the Russian defenders for wing wizard Willie Johnston to tuck away.

And despite the challenges of other goalkeepers like Stewart Kennedy, who also represented his country and was pressing for a first team place, McCloy kept goal on 644 occasions for Rangers, eclipsing the record of 545 appearances set by Gerry Dawson in the 1930s and 1940s. Surprisingly, he was capped only four times by Scotland and each time in 1973, against Wales (2-0), Northern Ireland (1-2), Switzerland (0-1) and Brazil (0-1).

Ally McCoist

PERSONAL FILE

Born: 24 September 1962
Birthplace: Bellshill
Height: 5' 10"
Weight: 12st 0lb

LEAGUE RECORD

FROM-TO	CLUB	APPS	GOALS
1978-81	St Johnstone	57	22
1981-83	Sunderland	56	8
1983-97	Rangers	402	245
Total		515	275

RANGERS LEAGUE DEBUT

20 August 1983 v St Mirren

SCOTLAND DEBUT

29 April 1986 v Holland

SCOTLAND HONOURS

SEASON	CAPS
1985-86	1
1986-87	5
1987-88	6
1988-89	4
1989-90	10
1990-91	5
1991-92	10
1992-93	5
1993-94	—
1994-95	—
1995-96	8
1996-97	4
Total	58

DID YOU KNOW?

Ally became known as Dudley after allegedly being labelled 'a dud' by Ibrox boss Graeme Souness.

As Rangers completed a decade of greatness by winning a ninth Scottish Premier Division title, the central character of their epic story was surely epitomised by that great scallywag of the goal-scoring fraternity, Ally McCoist.

Initially at St Johnstone and having failed in English football with Sunderland as a youngster, McCoist was just warming up, with his first 60-odd goals under his belt, when he won his first cap for Scotland in 1986 and helped Rangers to their first title since 1978 in the following season. He tucked away 33 goals in 39 League games that year and a further 31 in 40 as Rangers finished third in 1987-88. But in Graeme Souness' final season, despite Rangers clinching the title, McCoist had a barren year, scoring nine goals and playing only 18 League games. To say the centre-forward's relationship with his manager was frosty might be understating the case.

A Scotland regular, McCoist managed better than a goal a game in the next two seasons, as Walter Smith guided them to more Championship glory. Then he really exploded, scoring 34 goals in each of the 1991-92 and 1992-93 title seasons.

A broken leg in 1993 threatened to take the gloss off his later years, but to his credit McCoist, as irrepressible as ever, bounced back in 1995-96 in his 34th year with his best goalscoring form for three years.

A place in the European Championship squad was attained and, at long last, he surpassed Bob McPhail's 233-goal, 57-year-old record to become Rangers' leading League scorer of all time. Nor is the story over yet...

'To break Mr McPhail's record means more
to me than any other honour...
I don't think it will be broken.'

Ron McKinnon

PERSONAL FILE

Born: 20 August 1940
Birthplace: Glasgow
Height: 5' 10"
Weight: 10st 10lb

LEAGUE RECORD

FROM-TO	CLUB	APPS	GOALS
1961-72	Rangers	301	2

RANGERS LEAGUE DEBUT

8 March 1961 v Hearts

SCOTLAND DEBUT

9 November 1965 v Italy

SCOTLAND HONOURS

SEASON	CAPS
1965-66	6
1966-67	3
1967-68	4
1968-69	4
1969-70	6
1970-71	5
Total	28

Considered by many as the best centre-half ever to play in a Rangers strip, Ron McKinnon was the lynchpin of the solid defence of a team destined to play second fiddle to Celtic throughout the 1960s. Not only was he part of a mean club defence, he also reproduced this high level of play for his country and received 28 caps for Scotland.

Born in Glasgow, McKinnon played his football with various local youth sides before being signed by Rangers in 1959. He originally adopted an attacking midfield role, but first took on the responsibilities of centre-half to cover for injuries, and quickly found that the composure and authority he projected on the pitch suited this position perfectly. Natural skill, a great deal of practice and playing alongside other stalwarts like Harold Davis and Bobby Shearer meant that he quickly became proficient in the position and made it his own.

Success followed his move into the back four and Rangers, with the best defence in the League, began to close the gap on the ruling Celtic team. They followed the League and Scottish Cup Double in 1962-63 with the Treble the following year. This helped give Ron two League Championships, four Scottish Cups and three League Cups during his Ibrox career.

He would have also added a European Cup Winners' Cup medal to this tally had he been fit to play in the side which won the trophy in 1972. Unfortunately, he'd broken his leg the previous year in a European match and was unable to play a part in the Cup-winning side.

This injury effectively signalled the closing stages of McKinnon's time with Rangers. He left the club after the end of the next season and moved abroad to rekindle his world-class form. He spent the 1973-74 season in South Africa before moving further south to play his football in Australia.

DID YOU KNOW?
His twin brother Donald was centre-half with Partick Thistle between 1959-73.

Alan McLaren

PERSONAL FILE

Born: 4 January 1971
Birthplace: Edinburgh
Height: 5' 11"
Weight: 11st 6lb

LEAGUE RECORD

FROM-TO	CLUB	APPS	GOALS
1987-94	Hearts	182	6
1994-97	Rangers	78	5
Total		260	11

RANGERS LEAGUE DEBUT
30 October 1994 v Celtic

SCOTLAND DEBUT
17 May 1992 v USA

SCOTLAND HONOURS

SEASON	CAPS
1991-92	3
1992-93	5
1993-94	4
1994-95	9
1995-96	3
1996-97	—
Total	24

STAR QUOTE
'Alan has all the qualities that will make him a first-class captain of Scotland.'
WALTER SMITH

Alan McLaren is a born leader who, since his arrival in 1994, has become one of the key players at Ibrox. His ability to lead the defensive line has made him a firm favourite among the Rangers fans. He broke through to the Hearts first team in 1988 and became the brightest prospect at Tynecastle for years. McLaren stayed with Hearts for eight seasons and, when he decided he would quit the Edinburgh side, Rangers were always favourites to land the defender.

He signed for £1.5 million in 1994 and quickly established himself as a solid rock at the back. Richard Gough was the ideal partner for McLaren and the duo proved to be a difficult act for opposing forwards to deal with.

Always regarded as the natural successor to the Rangers' captaincy, his progress was hindered by a succession of knee injuries. National manager Craig Brown has also been disappointed by his lack of appearances for Scotland through injury.

And there was more bad news in the summer of 1997: just as the departure of Richard Gough to Kansas City Wiz meant McLaren was to become the mainstay of the defence, a serious knee injury ruled him out for seven months.

However, if he can regain his fitness, McLaren could yet go on to become as vital a figure for Rangers as had Gough.

Tommy McLean

DID YOU KNOW?
The McLeans were a footballing family: two older brothers played professionally before becoming managers.

The diminutive Tommy McLean joined Rangers in 1971 for a fee of £65,000, spending 11 seasons at the club before retiring to go into football management.

At five foot four inches, the new signing from Kilmarnock was a seasoned international with a touch on the ball as delicate as a virtuoso guitarist. McLean had been enticed to Ibrox by manager Willie Waddell, who knew his latest capture very well. Waddell had recruited the brilliant McLean as a youngster during his extremely successful time with Killie.

The outside-right was obviously under close scrutiny at Ibrox and was compared to former wing favourites like Willie Henderson and, of course, the manager himself. Yet he was not a demonstrative player like Henderson, nor did he not go on mazy runs or blast the ball with ballistic velocity like Alex Scott. What he did have was the ability to see a lateral opportunity and place the ball with incredible accuracy on the foot of goalscorers like Derek Parlane, Derek Johnstone or the robust Alex McDonald.

McLean enjoyed many of Rangers' great successes in the 1970s, particularly the 1972 European Cup Winners' Cup success over highly-rated Moscow Dynamo in Barcelona. He retired in 1982 after the 4-1 setback in the Scottish Cup Final against Aberdeen, having played almost 450 times in all competitions for Rangers. McLean then moved 'upstairs' and became assistant to manager John Greig and was caretaker for a while after Greig left. In 1984 he departed to spend ten years at Motherwell, where he enjoyed great success as a manager and, for a while sat on the board, before leaving Fir Park to take charge of Hearts.

McLean is currently in charge of Dundee United and, in their first season back in the Premier Division (1996-97), steered them to a highly-creditable third position in the table behind Rangers and Celtic.

1980-1988 & 1992-1994

Dave McPherson

PERSONAL FILE

Born: 28 January 1964
Birthplace: Paisley
Height: 6' 3"
Weight: 11st 11lb

LEAGUE RECORD

FROM-TO	CLUB	APPS	GOALS
1980-88	Rangers	205	19
1988-92	Hearts	145	12
1992-94	Rangers	71	3
1995-97	Hearts	52	2
Total		473	36

RANGERS LEAGUE DEBUT
9 October 1982 v Morton

SCOTLAND DEBUT
26 April 1989 v Cyprus

SCOTLAND HONOURS

SEASON	CAPS
1988-89	2
1989-90	5
1990-91	5
1991-92	11
1992-93	4
Total	27

STAR QUOTE
'A lot was made of the fact that fans didn't like me, but I think that was exaggerated.'

Dave McPherson is one of the few players to have enjoyed two spells at Rangers. The big centre-half, who had the unfortunate habit of appearing clumsy at times, first left the club for Hearts in 1988, then returned four years later. After another three years at Ibrox he was back at Tynecastle.

He first came to the attention of Rangers fans when he made his debut at 19. The young defender shone In one of the poorest sides in recent times and was deservedly voted Player of the Year by the supporters. However, his days at Ibrox were numbered when Graeme Souness arrived. Yet far from falling away, he blossomed in Edinburgh away from the pressure of being a Rangers player.

Walter Smith bought him back for £1 million and he was part of that great 1992-93 side which won the Treble and almost got to the European Cup Final. But after just nine games of the 1994-95 League season he was on his way again, a makeweight in the deal that brought Alan McLaren to Glasgow.

Always a threat at set-pieces due to his height, McPherson was occasionally given a hard time by fans, and sometimes suffered from being played at right-back – never his true position. Nevertheless, 'Big Slim' proved himself a consummate professional, and is known as one of the true gentlemen of the Scottish game.

1920-1933

Alan Morton

DID YOU KNOW?
Having already played nearly seven years at Hampden, Alan Morton spent two decades in top-flight football.

One of the greatest – some would say the greatest – player to wear the famous blue jersey of Rangers, Alan Morton remained a part-time athlete all through his dazzling career at Ibrox. Alan Lauder Morton, who was born in Glasgow in 1893, joined Rangers from Queen's Park in 1920 to replace the famous left-winger Dr Jim Paterson, who moved to further his medical career in London. Morton's reputation was already assured before leaving the Spiders for Ibrox, as he had won caps against Wales and Northern Ireland.

Morton was a mining engineer and remained so in spite of his incredible success with Rangers. A brilliant footballer, his fame among the football fans of the 1920s and 1930s was on a par with that of George Best in the 1960s or Alan Shearer today.

In spite of his diminutive frame – he stood at just five feet five inches and weighed just over ten stone wet through – Morton was a brilliant player with dribbling skills to marvel at. Furthermore, his balance was marvellous, allowing him to alter direction in an instant, a feature that bamboozled even the most gifted of defenders!

But Morton was from a gentler age and his nickname 'wee blue devil' was attributed to an England supporter at Wembley, who had become increasingly frustrated by the mercurial Morton's teasing of his side's defence. It is just possible that today's response from the crowd would be slightly less repeatable.

Morton retired at the end of the 1932-33 season and became a director until shortly before he died in 1971. He had played 498 games for Rangers and scored 166 goals, and won nine League Championships in 13 years. His spirit looms large still at Ibrox with his portrait, resplendent in a Rangers kit, a famous feature in the hall.

1983-1984 & 1986-1989

Jimmy Nicholl

PERSONAL FILE

Born: 28 February 1956
Birthplace: Hamilton, Canada
Height: 5' 10"
Weight: 11st 10lb

LEAGUE RECORD

FROM-TO	CLUB	APPS	GOALS
1974-81	Manchester Utd	197	3
1981-82	Sunderland (loan)	3	—
1982	Toronto Blizzard	16	3
1982-83	Sunderland	29	—
1983-84	Toronto Blizzard	49	8
1983-84	Rangers	17	—
1984-86	West Brom	56	—
1986-89	Rangers	65	—
1989-90	Dunfermline Ath	24	—
1990-95	Raith R	128	7
Total		584	21

RANGERS LEAGUE DEBUT
29 October 1983 v St Mirren

NORTHERN IRELAND DEBUT
3 March 1976 v Israel

NORTHERN IRELAND HONOURS

SEASON	CAPS
1975-76	2
1976-77	6
1977-78	6
1978-79	9
1979-80	9
1980-81	6
1981-82	10
1982-83	8
1983-84	5
1984-85	5
1985-86	7
Total	73

DID YOU KNOW?
Nicholl has played in both Manchester and Glasgow derbies.

One of the most likeable characters to play for Rangers, the softly-spoken Ulsterman made his name playing for Manchester United. Tommy Docherty made sure Nicholl was a fixture in the Old Trafford side of the late 1970s and he amassed numerous caps for Northern Ireland. Nicholl was transferred to Sunderland in 1981, but failed to hit it off at Roker Park.

He moved to Canada – his birthplace – for a spell with Toronto Blizzard before his first season at Ibrox in 1983 where he made 17 appearances, before moving south again to West Brom. Graeme Souness brought Nicholl back to Ibrox and he established himself under his Ibrox revolution. Nicholl was a versatile player who could play both in his preferred role of midfield or defence.

However, it was as a manager that he perhaps became more famous, when he became boss of Raith Rovers. He guided them to a famous Coca-Cola Cup triumph against Celtic at Ibrox in 1994 before embarking on a legendary European run that saw the Kirkcaldy club go a goal up against mighty Bayern Munich before eventually losing 2–1.

He moved on to Millwall, before returning to Rovers in 1997 after he was sacked by the London club.

Derek Parlane

PERSONAL FILE

Born: 5 May 1953
Birthplace: Helensburgh
Height: 6' 0"
Weight: 12st 2lb

LEAGUE RECORD

FROM-TO	CLUB	APPS	GOALS
1971-80	Rangers	202	80
1980-83	Leeds Utd	50	10
1983	Hong Kong	n/k	n/k
1983-85	Manchester C	48	20
1985	Swansea C	21	3
1985-86	Hong Kong	n/k	n/k
1986-87	Rochdale	42	10
Total		363	123

RANGERS LEAGUE DEBUT

1 January 1971 v Falkirk

SCOTLAND DEBUT

12 May 1973 v Wales

SCOTLAND HONOURS

SEASON	CAPS
1972-73	3
1973-74	—
1974-75	7
1975-76	1
1976-77	1
Total	12

DID YOU KNOW?

Both Parlane's Scottish League Cup winner's medals, obtained in 1978 and 1979, were won as a substitute.

Having signed for Rangers from Queen's Park as a midfielder, six-footer Derek Parlane – the son of a former Ranger, Jimmy – was converted into a front-runner and made an immediate impact. He scored a goal in his Rangers debut, the home Cup Winners' Cup Semi-Final tie against Bayern Munich. But he was playing in place of captain John Greig, who returned for the Final.

His heading ability, plus the knack of finding the net from some impossible angles, brought him to the attention of the national selectors and after six Under-23 caps he won the first of double that number in the national side. Surprisingly, he only scored once in the darker blue.

A move to Leeds United in 1980 ended his decade at Ibrox, having notched two League titles, three Scottish Cup and two Scottish League Cup winners medals: his tally stood at 80 goals in just over 200 League games. Derek was unable to approach that remarkable strike rate in an Elland Road team, despite scoring on his debut, and was loaned to Hong Kong side Bulova for nine months.

In August 1983 he moved to Manchester City, ironically then under ex-Celt Billy McNeill (a man who knew his abilities at first hand), and this change of scene brought a noticeable change of fortune. But with the Maine Road side narrowly failing to make it to the top flight, he was on the road again the following season to play out his career with Swansea, Rochdale (under former Leeds playing colleague Eddie Gray), and once more in Hong Kong with North Shore FC.

Parlane remained south of the border on ending his playing career and was, at one time, a director of non-League Macclesfield Town.

Gordan Petric

PERSONAL FILE

Born: 30 July 1969
Birthplace: Belgrade, Yugoslavia
Height: 6' 2"
Weight: 13st 9lb

LEAGUE RECORD

FROM-TO	CLUB	APPS	GOALS
1993-95	Dundee Utd	60	3
1995-97	Rangers	59	3
Total		119	6

RANGERS LEAGUE DEBUT

26 August 1995 v Kilmarnock

YUGOSLAVIA HONOURS

Has been capped by his country at full level

STAR QUOTE

'I want to win medals, and this is the place to do it.'

Gordan Petric has become something of an unsung hero during his short career at Rangers. Known as the 'suave Slav', Petric's cool and unflustered defending has been a feature of Rangers' play since he moved from Dundee United in a £1 million deal in 1995. However, the full extent of his cultured play has sometimes been smothered in the Ibrox side's rough-and-ready style of defending.

Petric arrived on Scottish shores in 1993, when Ivan Golac brought the talented youngster from Partizan Belgrade to Tannadice for £600,000. He was the rock on which United built their Scottish

Cup success a year later, and 12 months after that, Walter Smith won a battle with Celtic to take the star to Ibrox.

Petric's more natural game was allowed to prosper after the move. At United, he was forced to be the strength as well as the brains in defence. However, with combative characters such as Richard Gough and Alan McLaren at Ibrox, the grit was provided elsewhere to allow Petric's guile to dominate his play.

Sometimes accused of being a little too casual under pressure, Petric has his detractors among the Ibrox faithful. But Smith rarely leaves a fit Petric out of his starting line-up, and people in the know are becoming more and more impressed with his continental approach. And with manager Smith looking increasingly to Europe as a measure of his side's success, Petric has a continuing part to play.

Graeme Souness

PERSONAL FILE

Born: 6 May 1953
Birthplace: Edinburgh
Height: 5' 11"
Weight: 12st 13lb

LEAGUE RECORD

FROM-TO	CLUB	APPS	GOALS
1970-73	Tottenham H	—	—
1973-78	Middlesbrough	176	22
1978-84	Liverpool	247	38
1984-86	Sampdoria	56	8
1986-90	Rangers	50	3
Total		529	71

RANGERS LEAGUE DEBUT

9 August 1986 v Hibernian

SCOTLAND DEBUT

30 October 1974 v East Germany

SCOTLAND HONOURS

SEASON	CAPS
1974-75	3
1975-76	—
1976-77	—
1977-78	4
1978-79	5
1979-80	5
1980-81	3
1981-82	8
1982-83	9
1983-84	3
1984-85	7
1985-86	7
Total	54

DID YOU KNOW?

During his last game, his Ibrox team-mates tried to keep the ball away from him as long as possible!

The fiery-tempered and often irascible Graeme Souness will justifiably be credited as the catalyst for the revolution that changed the fortunes and outlook of Rangers beyond all recognition in the mid-1980s. Though he has not yet earned the devoted following that other managers like Bill Shankly, Sir Matt Busby or Brian Clough enjoyed, Souness' drive, vision and his achievements at Ibrox are nothing short of remarkable.

Souness became the first player-manager in the club's long history when, in April 1986, he was brought to Ibrox with a background of success that the then chairman, David Holmes, hoped would work in Govan. A born leader, Souness had won 54 caps for Scotland, becoming its captain, and had enjoyed incredible success with Liverpool sides in the 1970s and 1980s as well as World Cup campaigns with his country.

Holmes had lured Souness back to Britain from Sampdoria and gave him large sums of money with which to bring in players of proven ability. His first two major signings were England internationals goalkeeper Chris Woods from Norwich and defender Terry Butcher from Ipswich Town.

Souness secured the club's first Championship for nine years, leading his side to four titles and four League Cup successes in his five-year spell at Ibrox. Equally importantly, he persuaded David Murray to wrestle control from the John Lawrence consortium and the rest, as they say, is history.

Souness left in the spring of 1991 to return to Anfield as manager of Liverpool and, after a typically abrupt press conference, Murray observed, correctly, that he would regret doing so. He lasted two years in Merseyside, winning the FA Cup, but this time his spending power did not restore Liverpool to the great power in the land that Rangers became and have stayed. He later went on to manage Galatasaray (Turkey) and Southampton before taking charge of Italians Torino in 1997.

'I know in my own mind that I could never contemplate leaving Ibrox.'

1968-1972 & 1975-1978

Colin Stein

DID YOU KNOW?

Hotshot Stein scored eight goals in his first three matches in a Rangers shirt, including two hat-tricks.

One of the great Ibrox goalscorers, Colin Stein will always have a special place in the hearts of Rangers fans. Stein made a real impression when he was at Hibs, and that brought him to the attention of the Rangers management. The Ibrox club splashed out a record £100,000 plus winger Quinton Young to bring him to Glasgow – the first six-figure transfer in Scotland.

Stein made an immediate impact at Ibrox and established a rapport with the faithful, averaging more than a goal every other League game.

His scoring exploits included a four-goal haul for Scotland in a World Cup qualifying tie against Cyprus at Hampden Park in 1968. But his finest moment came in 1972 when he scored in the European Cup Winners' Cup Final against Moscow Dynamo in the Nou Camp Stadium. His scoring record during the tournament was superb, netting four goals in two games against Sporting Lisbon, and shrugging off the challenge of the Dynamo defence, before crashing an unstoppable shot past the keeper to send Rangers on their way to a famous 3–2 triumph.

At Coventry, he aided an ailing side to hold on to their top-flight status and enjoy a Sixth Round FA Cup run. Never as prolific at Highfield Road, Stein soon found himself on his way back to Ibrox as the Sky Blues sold to survive. Unfortunately, he could not reproduce his earlier form for the club and he retired in the 1978 close season after a loan spell at Kilmarnock.

Powerfully built, strong and exceptionally brave in the penalty box, Stein had all the qualities that make a great striker. He is now working as a carpet fitter and is a keen bowler.

1989-1991 & 1992-1997

Trevor Steven

PERSONAL FILE

Born: 21 September 1963
Birthplace: Berwick
Height: 5' 8"
Weight: 10st 9lb

LEAGUE RECORD

FROM-TO	CLUB	APPS	GOALS
1980-83	Burnley	76	11
1983-89	Everton	214	48
1989-91	Rangers	55	6
1991-92	Marseille	27	3
1992-97	Rangers	81	10
Total		453	78

RANGERS LEAGUE DEBUT

12 August 1989 v St Mirren

ENGLAND DEBUT

27 February 1985 v Northern Ireland

ENGLAND HONOURS

SEASON	CAPS
1984-85	6
1985-86	7
1986-87	3
1987-88	8
1988-89	1
1989-90	4
1990-91	1
1991-92	6
Total	36

DID YOU KNOW?
On being granted a free transfer in summer 1997, Trevor Steven had trials with Hearts.

Rangers' success may traditionally have been built around hard work and commitment, but Trevor Steven didn't fit the usual Ibrox stereotype. An elegant and cultured midfielder, he brought a new dimension to the side when he signed from Everton in 1989. His ability on the ball was superb and he created countless chances for the strikers with his superb vision and clever passing.

Steven began his career at Burnley, where he spent three seasons before joining Everton. He became a key part of arguably the greatest Goodison team ever, winning League Championships, the FA Cup and European Cup Winners' Cup. So it was seen as a massive coup for Rangers when Graeme Souness snapped him up for £1.5 million in 1989. Steven dazzled the Ibrox fans in that first season and capped a wonderful campaign with the winning goal against Dundee United at Tannadice to clinch the League title.

He then turned in impressive performances for England in the World Cup in Italy in 1990 and returned for another excellent term at Ibrox. That form attracted attention from around Europe, and French champions Marseille snatched Steven for a hefty £5.5 million. However, his spell in the south of France was not successful, and he returned to Rangers for £2.5 million a year later. Unfortunately, Steven then began to suffer injury problems and his runs

in the first team were limited. With Paul Gascoigne now occupying his place in the side, Steven was labelled surplus to requirements at Ibrox.

Gary Stevens

LEAGUE RECORD

FROM-TO	CLUB	APPS	GOALS
1980-88	Everton	208	8
1988-94	Rangers	187	8
1994-97	Tranmere	102	1
Total		497	17

RANGERS LEAGUE DEBUT
13 August 1988 v Hamilton Athletic

ENGLAND DEBUT
6 June 1985 v Italy

ENGLAND HONOURS

SEASON	CAPS
1984-85	2
1985-86	12
1986-87	2
1987-88	10
1988-89	7
1989-90	8
1990-91	1
1991-92	4
Total	46

DID YOU KNOW?
During his England career, Gary played four times against Scotland and was never on the losing side.

Gary Stevens' name may not instantly come to mind when people speak of Rangers legends. But the powerful defender was influential in putting Rangers on the road to making history! Stevens arrived from Everton, fresh from collecting League, FA Cup and European Cup Winners' Cup medals at Goodison, in a £1 million deal in 1988. Little did he or any Rangers fans realise the significance of a goal on his debut at Hamilton on 13 August – the opening day of the campaign.

Stevens scored Rangers' first goal in a 2–0 win at Douglas Park and Graeme Souness' side marched on to collect the Championship that season. Nine years later, Rangers had completed the incredible nine-in-a-row feat to equal Celtic's record – and Stevens was the man who had started the ball rolling. He played a significant part in the run and only Richard Gough made more appearances in the nine seasons than did Stevens.

His popularity among fans did fall slightly when his dreadfully short back-pass allowed Celtic's Joe Miller to snatch the only goal of the 1989 Cup Final – denying Rangers a Treble. Even so, he continued to clock up the games – well over 200 in all competitions – and survived much longer than his contemporaries form south of the border.

Sold to Tranmere for £350,000 in 1994, Stevens never recaptured former glories, but his achievements at Ibrox still rank high.

1938-1955

Willie Waddell

PERSONAL FILE

Born: 7 March 1921
Birthplace: Forth
Died: 13 October 1992
Height: 5' 10"
Weight: 12st 2lb

LEAGUE RECORD

FROM-TO	CLUB	APPS	GOALS
1938-55	Rangers	196	37

RANGERS LEAGUE DEBUT

3 September 1938 v Ayr United

SCOTLAND DEBUT

9 October 1946 v Wales

SCOTLAND HONOURS

SEASON	CAPS
1946-47	1
1947-48	—
1948-49	4
1949-50	2
1950-51	5
1951-52	2
1952-53	—
1953-54	1
1954-55	2
Total	17

DID YOU KNOW?
Waddell's Kilmarnock team faced Rangers in both League and FA Cup Finals of 1960, losing each time.

Willie Waddell's immense contribution to Rangers history is usually viewed from the context of his career as manager. Older readers will recall, however, that he'd written his name in the Ibrox record books during his career as a solidly-built, powerful right-winger between 1938 and 1955. Much of his career took place in wartime and is thus not to be found in the official record books: in total, it's reckoned that Waddell may have registered some 558 matches and 143 goals, figures which dwarf the League statistics recorded here.

Having made his international debut in late 1946, he was then overlooked for a season before returning to the Scotland side for more of an extended run. Again, war robbed him of more impressive figures, five wartime internationals counting for nothing in the record books. At Rangers, his centres were the source of many goals for Willie Thornton and an expectant murmur would go up every time Waddell gained possession.

On leaving Ibrox in the summer of 1956, he took a year to get his first managerial post at Kilmarnock, and took the Rugby Park side to an unheard-of Championship in 1965. After retiring at the peak of his success to become a working journalist, he was summoned to take the reins from the unfortunate David White, an unsuccessful successor to long-serving Scot Symon. He steadied the ship and reigned from 1969 to 1972, when he ceded team affairs to his younger lieutenant, Jock Wallace. But his job as general manger was no sinecure and he was much in evidence in the drawn-out aftermath of the Ibrox Disaster of 1971, when safety considerations laid the foundations for today's ground.

Waddell resigned as managing director and vice chairman in 1979, but remained associated with the club as a director and consultant. He died in 1992, but his name has been commemorated in Ibrox's 'Waddell Suite'.

1987-1989

Ray Wilkins

Cruelly and erroneously named 'The Crustacean' by former Manchester United manager Ron Atkinson, Ray Wilkins is probably one of the most skilful midfielders to have worn the famous blue jersey. Atkinson's none-too-serious jibe, coined because of Wilkins' liking for the lateral pass, disguises the Hillingdon-born player's brilliant creative skills which have been paraded at the highest level.

Wilkins' potential was recognised very early in his career when, as a 21-year-old, he was given the captaincy of his first club, Chelsea. In spite of the nickname 'Butch', his maturity and patience was a byword among his fellow professionals.

The elegant Londoner left in 1979, after six years at Stamford Bridge, for Manchester United, where he stayed for five seasons, gracing the FA Cup-winning side of 1983. Wilkins' svelte skills and ice-cool temperament then attracted AC Milan and Paris St Germain, for whom he played until Rangers manager Graeme Souness signed him for an unbelievably cheap £250,000 in 1987.

Although his career at Ibrox lasted only two years, he became a great favourite with the Rangers faithful, who recognised a great talent. But in that spell he helped the club lift the Championship and the League Cup in 1988-89.

Souness' hunch that Wilkins, whom he knew well, would turn out to be a diamond for Rangers, was remarkably astute. Nearly all of the play went through Wilkins and, when at times the play was fast and furious, his panache was applauded to the rafters at Ibrox. He played for the last time in the famous blue jersey in November 1989.

Capped 84 times for his country, Wilkins returned to his beloved London in 1989 to join Queens Park Rangers, whom he later managed, bringing in Mark Hateley from his old club.

1986-1991

Chris Woods

PERSONAL FILE

Born: 14 November 1959
Birthplace: Boston
Height: 6' 2"
Weight: 14st 12lb

LEAGUE RECORD

FROM-TO	CLUB	APPS	GOALS
1976-79	Nott'm Forest	—	—
1979-80	QPR	63	—
1980-86	Norwich C	216	—
1986-91	Rangers	173	—
1991-95	Sheffield Wed	107	—
1995	Reading (loan)	5	—
1996-97	Southampton	4	—
Total		568	—

RANGERS LEAGUE DEBUT

9 August 1986 v Hibernian

ENGLAND DEBUT

16 June 1985 v USA

ENGLAND HONOURS

SEASON	CAPS
1984-85	1
1985-86	3
1986-87	5
1987-88	4
1988-89	1
1989-90	2
1990-91	8
1991-92	10
1992-93	9
Total	43

STAR QUOTE

Though he never made a League appearance for Forest, Woods was a member of the side that won the 1978 League Cup.

74

Graeme Souness' second big-name signing after Terry Butcher when he started the Ibrox revolution in 1986, Woods was an extremely capable goalkeeper who enjoyed a highly successful career at both club and international level.

His first season at Ibrox went like a dream when he won the Skol Cup and Premier League title, and also broke the British shut-out record. He would have picked up a lot more than his 43 England caps if it hadn't been for Peter Shilton, but he did play in the 1992 European Championships. Woods benefited from playing behind a defence of Butcher and Richard Gough, but when he was called into action few forwards managed to beat him. His greatest game as a Rangers player was probably his last, when a 2–0 win over Aberdeen at Ibrox in a title decider secured yet another Championship.

Woods must have felt his career at Rangers was safe, but when Walter Smith took over from Graeme Souness, Woods was on his way to Sheffield Wednesday to make way for Andy Goram. After four successful seasons at Hillsborough, he joined the exodus to the US Soccer Federation. Souness brought him back to Britain in 1996 when he signed him for Southampton, only for Woods to break his leg within weeks of his arrival at the Dell.

Both a solid and, when required, spectacular goalkeeper, this popular Englishman will always have a special place in the hearts of Rangers fans who enjoyed the luxury of watching him.

George Young

PERSONAL FILE

Born: 27 October 1922
Birthplace: Grangemouth
Height: 6' 2"
Weight: 15st 0lb

LEAGUE RECORD

FROM-TO	CLUB	APPS	GOALS
1946-57	Rangers	293	22

RANGERS LEAGUE DEBUT

10 August 1946 v Motherwell

SCOTLAND DEBUT

27 April 1946 v Northern Ireland

SCOTLAND HONOURS

SEASON	CAPS
1946-47	4
1947-48	5
1948-49	4
1949-50	6
1950-51	8
1951-52	6
1952-53	4
1953-54	2
1954-55	4
1955-56	4
1956-57	6
Total	53

DID YOU KNOW:

Young was nicknamed 'Corky' due to his superstition of carrying a lucky champagne cork on the pitch.

A major cornerstone of Rangers' so-called 'Iron Curtain' defence, George Lewis Young had recorded 110 games and 14 goals in World War II before making his full Rangers League debut. So certain of his ability were Rangers that they signed him on amateur forms at the age of just 15.

Initially a centre-half, he moved to right-back when Willie Woodburn arrived and excelled in either role. Right-footed, his ability to kick the ball the whole length of the pitch was legendary, while his ball-winning on the ground and his dominance in the air made him the complete defender. A lack of mobility, given his immense height and weight, was his only Achilles heel.

National honours came thick and fast, and as a born leader he was a natural choice to captain his country. His 53 caps included 48 as skipper (then a record), while he also set records both for number of caps won and consecutive games. His gigantic stature was far from purely physical.

The 'Iron Curtain' defence was based on a near ever-present formation from keeper Brown through to left-half Cox. In consecutive seasons, 1948-50, the six players concerned missed just seven appearances between them – testament to a fitness and temperament which

Young epitomised.

His Ibrox career saw him win six titles and six Cups – four FA, two League – to leave him with a mantlepiece full of honours. On retiring from playing in May 1957, he returned to the game two years later as manager of Third Lanark. That spell lasted some three years before he opted for life as a hotelier.

Top 20 League Appearances
(of the players featured in this book)

1	John Greig	1961-78	496
2	Sandy Jardine	1967-82	417
3	Ally McCoist	1983-97	402
4	Alan Morton	1920-33	382
5	Davie Cooper	1977-89	377
6	Derek Johnstone	1970-83 & 1985-86	375
7	Peter McCloy	1970-86	351
8	Colin Jackson	1963-82	343
9	Alex McDonald	1968-80	306
10	Ron McKinnon	1961-72	301
11	Tommy McLean	1971-82	300
12	Richard Gough	1987-97	294
13	George Young	1946-57	293
14	Willie Henderson	1961-72	276
14	Dave McPherson	1980-88 & 1992-94	276
16	Eric Caldow	1953-66	265
17	Willie Johnston	1964-72 & 1980-82	246
18	Iain Durrant	1984-97	240
19	Tom Forsyth	1972-82	220
20	Ian Ferguson	1988-97	211

Right: A familiar scene as Ally McCoist is mobbed following another successful strike.

League Cup Record 1968-97 – The Highs and Lows

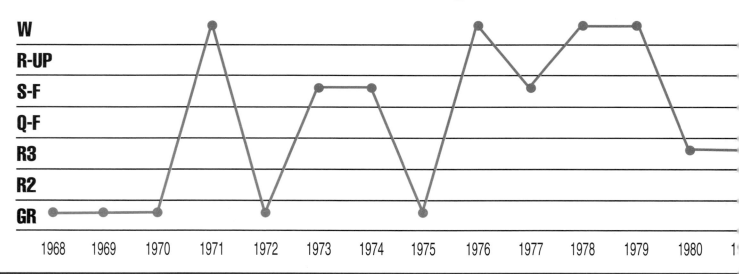

Top 20 League Scorers
(of the players featured in this book)

1	Ally McCoist	1983-97	245
2	Derek Johnstone	1970-83 & 1985-86	122
3	Willie Johnston	1964-72 & 1980-82	91
4	John Greig	1961-78	87
5	Mark Hateley	1990-95 & 1996-97	86
6	Alan Morton	1920-33	83
7	Derek Parlane	1971-80	80
8	Colin Stein	1968-72 & 1975-78	64
9	Alex McDonald	1968-80	51
10	Davie Cooper	1977-89	49
11	Willie Waddell	1938-55	37
12	Willie Henderson	1961-72	36
13	Tommy McLean	1971-82	34
14	Sandy Jardine	1967-82	33
15	Brian Laudrup	1994-97	28
16	Paul Gascoigne	1995-97	27
17	Iain Durrant	1984-97	26
18	Richard Gough	1987-97	25
19	Colin Jackson	1963-82	23
20	Ian Ferguson	1988-97	22
20	Dave McPherson	1980-88 & 1992-94	22
20	George Young	1946-57	22

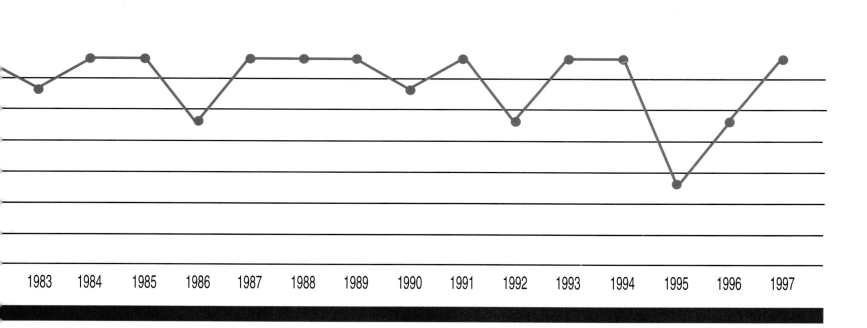

1983 1984 1985 1986 1987 1988 1989 1990 1991 1992 1993 1994 1995 1996 1997

League Record 1968-97

DIVISION ONE							
Season	Pos	Pts	F-A	1980-81	3rd	44	60-32
1967-68	2nd	61	93-34	1981-82	3rd	43	57-45
1968-69	2nd	49	81-32	1982-83	4th	38	52-41
1969-70	2nd	45	67-40	1983-84	4th	42	53-41
1970-71	4th	41	58-34	1984-85	4th	38	47-38
1971-72	3rd	44	71-38	1985-86	5th	35	53-45
1972-73	2nd	56	74-30	1986-87	1st	69	85-23
1973-74	3rd	48	67-34	1987-88	3rd	60	85-34
1974-75	1st	56	86-33	1988-89	1st	56	62-26
				1989-90	1st	51	48-19
				1990-91	1st	55	62-23
PREMIER DIVISION				1991-92	1st	72	101-31
Season	Pos	Pts	F-A	1992-93	1st	73	97-35
1975-76	1st	54	60-24	1993-94	1st	58	74-41
1976-77	2nd	46	62-37	*Introduction of three points per win*			
1977-78	1st	55	76-39	1994-95	1st	69	60-35
1978-79	2nd	45	52-35	1995-96	1st	87	85-25
1979-80	5th	37	50-46	1996-97	1st	80	85-33

Right: Derek McInnes celebrates scoring against Dunfermline.

Left: Gordon Durie, scorer of a hat-trick as Hearts were thrashed 5-1 in the 1996 FA Cup Final.

FA Cup Record 1968-97 – The Highs and Lows

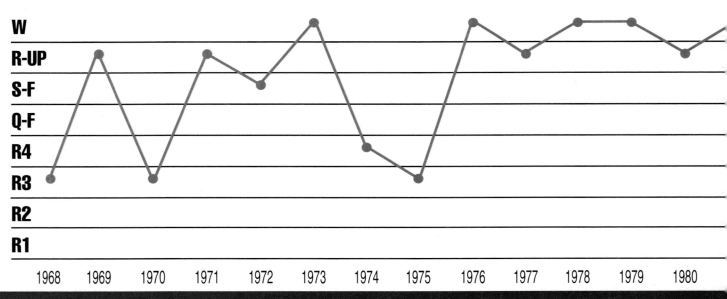

FA Cup Milestones 1968-97 *(see details of Highs & Lows below)*

Season	Opponents	Score	Season	Opponents	Score
1967-68	Hearts	1-1, 0-1	1982-83	Aberdeen	0-1
1968-69	Celtic	0-4	1983-84	Dundee	2-2, 2-3
1969-70	Celtic	1-3	1984-85	Dundee	0-1
1970-71	Celtic	1-1, 1-2	1985-86	Hearts	2-3
1971-72	Hibernian	1-1, 0-2	1986-87	Hamilton Academicals	0-1
1972-73	Celtic	3-2	1987-88	Dunfermline Athletic	0-2
1973-74	Dundee	0-3	1988-89	Celtic	0-1
1974-75	Aberdeen	1-1, 1-2	1989-90	Celtic	0-1
1975-76	Hearts	3-1	1990-91	Celtic	0-2
1976-77	Celtic	0-1	1991-92	Airdrie	2-1
1977-78	Aberdeen	2-1	1992-93	Aberdeen	2-1
1978-79	Hibernian	0-0, 0-0, 3-2	1993-94	Dundee United	0-1
1979-80	Celtic	0-1	1994-95	Hearts	2-4
1980-81	Dundee United	0-0, 4-1	1995-96	Hearts	5-1
1981-82	Aberdeen	1-4	1996-97	Celtic	0-2

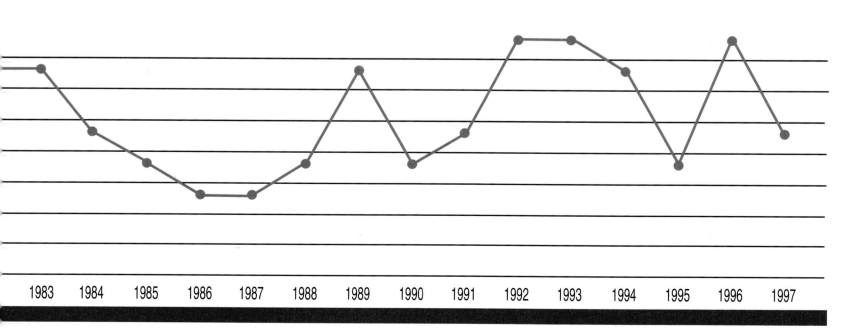

| 1983 | 1984 | 1985 | 1986 | 1987 | 1988 | 1989 | 1990 | 1991 | 1992 | 1993 | 1994 | 1995 | 1996 | 1997 |

Honours

1876-77	FA Cup Runners-up	1959-60	FA Cup Winners
1878-79	FA Cup Runners-up	1960-61	Division One Champions, League Cup Winners and European Cup Winners' Cup Runners-up
1890-91	Division One Champions (shared with Dumbarton)		
1892-93	Division One Runners-up	1961-62	Division One Runners-up, FA Cup Winners and League Cup Winners
1893-94	FA Cup Winners		
1895-96	Division One Runners-up		
1896-97	FA Cup Winners	1962-63	Division One Champions and FA Cup Winners
1897-98	Division One Runners-up and FA Cup Winners		
1898-99	Division One Champions and FA Cup Runners-up	1963-64	Division One Champions, FA Cup Winners and League Cup Winners
1899-1900	Division One Champions	1964-65	League Cup Winners
1900-01	Division One Champions	1965-66	Division One Runners-up, FA Cup Winners and League Cup Runners-up
1901-02	Division One Champions		
1902-03	FA Cup Winners	1966-67	Division One Runners-up, League Cup Runners-up and European Cup Winners' Cup Runners-up
1903-04	FA Cup Runners-up		
1904-05	Division One Runners-up and FA Cup Runners-up		
1910-11	Division One Champions	1967-68	Division One Runners-up
1911-12	Division One Champions	1968-69	Division One Runners-up and FA Cup Runners-up
1912-13	Division One Champions		
1913-14	Division One Runners-up	1969-70	Division One Runners-up
1915-16	Division One Runners-up	1970-71	FA Cup Runners-up and League Cup Winners
1917-18	Division One Champions		
1918-19	Division One Runners-up	1971-72	European Cup Winners' Cup Winners
1919-20	Division One Champions		
1920-21	Division One Champions and FA Cup Runners-up	1972-73	Division One Runners-up and FA Cup Winners
1921-22	Division One Runners-up and FA Cup Runners-up	1974-75	Division One Champions
		1975-76	Premier Division Champions, FA Cup Winners and League Cup Winners
1922-23	Division One Champions		
1923-24	Division One Champions		
1924-25	Division One Champions	1976-77	Premier Division Runners-up and FA Cup Runners-up
1926-27	Division One Champions		
1927-28	Division One Champions and FA Cup Winners	1977-78	Premier Division Champions, FA Cup Winners and League Cup Winners
1928-29	Division One Champions and FA Cup Runners-up		
1929-30	Division One Champions and FA Cup Winners	1978-79	Premier Division Runners-up, FA Cup Winners and League Cup Winners
1930-31	Division One Champions	1979-80	FA Cup Runners-up
1931-32	Division One Runners-up and FA Cup Winners	1980-81	FA Cup Winners
		1981-82	FA Cup Runners-up and League Cup Winners
1932-33	Division One Champions		
1933-34	Division One Champions and FA Cup Winners	1982-83	FA Cup Runners-up and League Cup Runners-up
1934-35	Division One Champions and FA Cup Winners	1983-84	League Cup Winners
		1984-85	League Cup Winners
1935-36	Division One Runners-up and FA Cup Winners	1986-87	Premier Division Champions and League Cup Winners
1936-37	Division One Champions	1987-88	League Cup Winners
1938-39	Division One Champions	1988-89	Premier Division Champions, FA Cup Runners-up and League Cup Winners
1946-47	Division One Champions and League Cup Winners		
1947-48	Division One Runners-up and FA Cup Winners	1989-90	Premier Division Champions and League Cup Runners-up
1948-49	Division One Champions, FA Cup Winners and League Cup Winners	1990-91	Premier Division Champions and League Cup Winners
		1991-92	Premier Division Champions and FA Cup Winners
1949-50	Division One Champions and FA Cup Winners		
1950-51	Division One Runners-up	1992-93	Premier Division Champions, FA Cup Winners and League Cup Winners
1951-52	Division One Runners-up and League Cup Runners-up		
1952-53	Division One Champions and FA Cup Winners	1993-94	Premier Division Champions, FA Cup Runners-up and League Cup Winners
1955-56	Division One Champions	1994-95	Premier Division Champions
1956-57	Division One Champions	1995-96	Premier Division Champions and FA Cup Winners
1957-58	Division One Runners-up and League Cup Runners-up		
		1996-97	Premier Division Champions and League Cup Winners
1958-59	Division One Champions		

Above: Paul Gascoigne helped Rangers to their 20th League Cup with two goals in the 1996-97 Final.